The Culture of
Learning Organizations

The Culture of Learning Organizations

Understanding Argyris' Theory through
a Socio-Cognitive Systems Learning Model

Laura Friesenborg, Ed.D., SPHR

Brennan-Mitchell Publishing Group

**Brennan-Mitchell
Publishing Group**

Forest City, Iowa

Library of Congress Cataloging-in-Publication Data

Friesenborg, Laura

    The Culture of Learning Organizations: Understanding Argyris' Theory through a

Socio-Cognitive Systems Learning Model / Laura Friesenborg.

        p. cm.

    Includes bibliographic references and index.

    ISBN: 978-0-9911607-0-9 (paperback); ISBN: 978-0-9911607-3-0 (e-book).

    1. Organization learning. 2. Organization culture. I. Title.

Printed in the United States of America

First Edition

For Lonnie,
with gratitude and love.

Contents

Tables

Figures

Acknowledgements

Thank you to Drs. John Conbere and Alla Heorhiadi for challenging and encouraging me, as well as introducing me to the work of Chris Argyris. I have learned so much from you, and I appreciate your wisdom and guidance.

Thank you to Dr. Mike Waggoner for introducing me to Parker Palmer's work and encouraging me to "let my life speak."

Most especially, thanks to Lonnie, Brennan, and Mitchell, Mom and Dad, Grandma, and Jeanne for all your love and encouragement. You are my greatest joy!

1

Organization Learning

"Human beings are designed for learning" (Senge, 2006b, p. 765).
"...yet most people don't know how to learn" (Argyris, 2006b, p. 267).

What does this paradox mean?

The human brain is innately wired to learn. Humans are created to derive pleasure from learning and to apply that learning as they interact with the world. Parker Palmer wrote, "We arrive in this world undivided, integral, whole. But sooner or later, we erect a wall between our inner and outer lives, trying to protect what is within us or to deceive the people around us" (Palmer, 2004, p. 39). "And I am sometimes moved to wonder, 'Whatever became of me?'" (Palmer, 2004, p. 40).

If humans are born "undivided, integral, whole" (Palmer, 2004, p. 39), what fractures that wholeness? Palmer suggested, "The instinct to protect ourselves by living divided lives emerges when we are young, as we start to see gaps between life's bright promise and its shadowy realities" (Palmer, 2004, p. 14). Recognizing such shadowy realities, W. Edwards Deming wrote, "Our prevailing system of management has destroyed our people...People are born with intrinsic motivation, self-esteem, dignity, curiosity to learn, joy in learning. The forces of destruction begin with toddlers—a prize for the best Halloween costume, grades in school, gold stars, and on up through the university. On the job, people, teams, divisions are ranked— reward for the one at the top, punishment at the bottom. Management by objectives, quotas, incentive pay, business plans, put together separately, division by division, cause further loss, unknown and unknowable" (Senge, 2006a, p. xii). "Ironically, by focusing on performing for someone else's approval, corporations create the very conditions that predestine them to mediocre performance" (Senge, 2006b, p. 766).

Compromising organization performance and riddling the organization with hidden costs (Conbere & Heorhiadi, 2011), the traditional corporate culture may damage people's sense of self (Argyris, 2000; Deming, as cited in Senge, 2006a; Palmer, 2004). Argyris (2010) said, "Individuals build a mind-set that they are victims of the system. They are helpless. But in reality we are not helpless" (p. 4). To heal, Palmer (2004) wrote, "Only when the pain of our dividedness becomes more clear than we can bear do most of us embark on an inner journey toward living 'divided no more'" (p. 39). On a societal level, healing may come in the form of learning and change among the culture's institutions, such as organizations (Bellah, Madsen, Sullivan, Swidler, & Tipton, 2008; Csikszentmihalyi, 2003; Kroeber & Kluckhohn, 1952, as cited in Adams & Markus, 2004; Palmer, 2004; Waggoner, 2011).

Argyris (2010) said, "The good news is that [the organization's] powerful traps can begin to be changed and reduced during relatively straightforward interventions that emphasize social and cognitive skills" (p. 4). Healing on an organization level requires organization learning and change. These occur when "each worker's potentialities find room for expression" (Csikszentmihalyi, 2003, p. 107), when the culture invites wholeness for each person (Palmer, 2004, 2011; Walsh, 2010). This approach is the hallmark of learning organizations.

What Is a Learning Organization?

Argyris and Schön (1996) defined a learning organization as an organization with the "ability to see things in new ways, gain new understandings, and produce new patterns of behavior—all on a continuing basis and in a way that engages the organization as a whole" (p. xix). Organization learning is not simply a plan for employees to learn tasks and procedures. It is more than expecting employees to comply with lean systems or continuous improvement strategies. Instead, the focus is creating a collaborative culture that provides psychological safety for people to ask questions, voice their recommendations, and challenge the way things have always been done (Edmondson, 2012). The emphasis is moved from management decision-making and employee compliance to a culture where leaders and employees have open discussion when decisions are made, and initiatives are co-created. Through this approach, the organization leverages the talents of individuals throughout the organization.

Organization learning was popularized with the 1990 release of Peter Senge's bestselling book, *The Fifth Discipline: The Art and Practice of the Learning Organization*. The book's release resulted in accolades throughout the business community and was heralded by *Harvard Business Review's* (HBR's) 75th anniversary issue as one of most influential books in HBR's history ("Seminal Management Books...," 1997). Despite the excitement generated by this book, the topic of organization learning remained largely conceptual. Theories related to organization learning were developed, yet rarely tested (Argyris & Schön, 1996).

Organization learning has been identified as a best practice and has been included in the strategic plans of countless organizations. Yet, the system of values, behaviors, and outcomes that create a culture of organization learning remains unclear.

Consistent with the dominant culture in the U.S., organizations continue to approach change efforts using task learning (Habermas, 1984, as cited in Mezirow, 2000; Mezirow, 2000, 2003). Organization learning is typically described by a list of prescriptive criteria that an organization must demonstrate in order to march in-step with "best practices" organizations. Employee engagement is often found at the top of that list of criteria and considered to be the primary performance indicator of organization learning. Despite the critical need to learn and change, organizations continue to approach organization learning as an add-on to their work, as a checklist of prescriptive "to do" items (Argyris, 2010).

Organizations are entrenched in the complex social system they are trying to understand, which may create blindness. Argyris and Schön (1996) described the predominant approach to organization learning—among both organization leaders and academic researchers—as exhibiting blindness toward the underlying functions that shape organization learning. These functions are the behavioral norms that reinforce, and are cyclically reinforced by, the organization's behavior patterns (Adams & Markus, 2004; Akün, Lynn, & Byrne, 2003; Bandura, 2002; Kitayama, Duffy,

& Uchida, 2007). Today, though lip-service is paid to organization learning, most organizations are fraught with systems and norms designed to control, blame, and inhibit learning (Argyris, 2000, 2004, 2006b, 2010). Organizations may be challenged to understand the organization learning process, much less take steps to change (Argyris & Schön, 1996; Edmondson, 1996).

This book is driven by the desire to help people lift the veils of blindness, to see the default pattern of dysfunction that humans practice as we interact with one another. Above all, this book is driven by a desire to show that there is an alternative. This alternative pattern of interaction honors the humanity of the organization and leads to wholeness and organization health. Once we are liberated from blindness, and we recognize the default pattern for its destruction, the choice becomes ours. Will we continue to perpetuate the culture-driven cycle of dysfunction, or will we influence the culture toward the alternative: honoring humanity and laying the foundation for change and innovation? The choice is ours. The choice is yours.

2

Socio-Cognitive
Systems Learning Model

The Socio-Cognitive Systems Learning Model was developed to help people understand the cultural default pattern of defensive, destructive human interaction within organizations and other social systems. The model compares this pattern of dysfunction with the alternative pattern of organization learning and change.

Focusing on the mental models that drive social behavior, the Socio-Cognitive Systems Learning Model was developed to diagram and build upon Argyris' (2000) theory of organization learning. A simplified version of the model was created (see Figure 1), in addition to the original model (see Figure 2). The elements of the model—the values, learned social behaviors, and outcomes of the contrasting cultural patterns of dysfunction (i.e., Model I) and organization learning (i.e., Model II)—will be discussed in subsequent chapters.

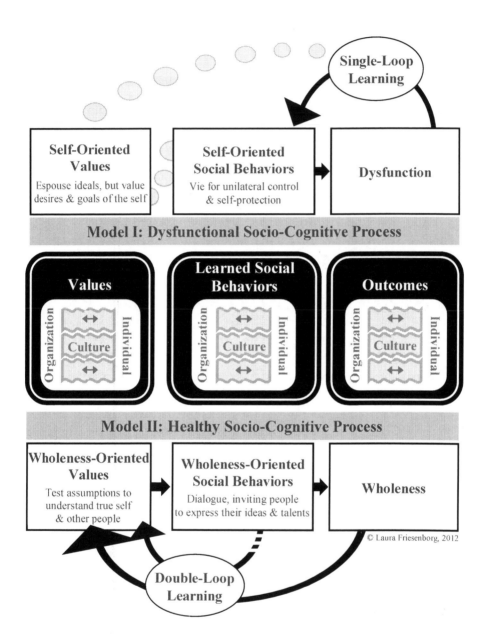

Figure 1. Socio-Cognitive Systems Learning Model: Simplified Version.

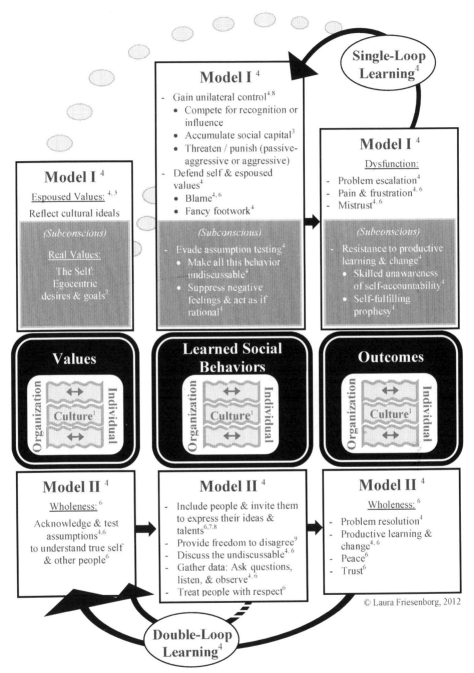

Figure 2. Socio-Cognitive Systems Learning Model.

Sources: [1] Adams & Markus, 2004; [2] Kitayama et al., 2007; [3] Bandura, 2002; [4] Argyris, 2000, 2004, 2010; Argyris & Schön, 1996; [5] Schein, 2009; [6] Mezirow, 2003; Palmer, 2004, 2011; [7] Csikszentmihalyi, 2003; [8] Walsh, 2010; [9] Brehm, 2009.

3

Organization Culture

"...Success in the marketplace increasingly depends on learning"
(Senge, 2006b, p. 267).

Attributing success to learning might sound like common sense. However, the American culture typically misinterprets "learning." Our culture tends to assume that "learning" means learning tasks and becoming an expert at those tasks. In contrast, success in the marketplace depends on organization learning. This means that we learn how to develop and sustain an organization culture with norms to reinforce open, respectful relationships among people on a team. Similarly, we learn how to develop and sustain open, respectful relationships *between* the teams that comprise the organization.

You might be thinking, "Even if I care about this, my manager and team members will dismiss this stuff as 'soft.' They won't care about how people get along and work together. They're focused exclusively on the bottom line." This perspective assumes that how people get along and work together is irrelevant—simply a "nice to have"—or, worse yet, it is considered "fluff." This perspective assumes that how people get along and work together is completely irrelevant to the bottom line.

On the contrary, how people get along and work together is *strongly* related to the bottom line. The typical organization is wrought with dysfunctional working relationships and silos that do two things: (a) generate expensive hidden costs for the organization and (b) obstruct the human potential that is essential for organization agility and innovation. For learning organizations, developing human potential and productive working relationships are not just "nice to haves." Instead, they are top priorities. Learning organizations recognize them as key drivers for success in the marketplace (Conbere & Heorhiadi, 2011; Cristallini & Savall, 2014; Heorhiadi, Conbere, & Hazelbaker, 2014; Edmondson, 2012; Garvin, Edmondson, & Gino, 2008).

So, if the organization culture—and, let's be honest, the dominant American society as a whole—considers human potential and productive working relationships as "soft," how do we change this perspective? How do we help people to recognize the assumption that "human potential and productive working relationships are irrelevant to the bottom line" actually creates blindness toward key drivers for organization success? How do we help people recognize that they are blind toward the very factors that would generate what managers value?

In other words, how do we help managers make the connection between: (a) human potential and productive working relationships, (b) the agility to change quickly to adapt to the market and the innovation to create new products or even create new markets, and (c) an enriched bottom line?

The answer to these questions is this: by influencing the organization culture. The first step is to understand how organization culture works.

How the Individual and the Organization
Influence Each Other through Culture

What comes to mind when you think of "culture?" Does music, film, fashion, or art come to mind? How about football, basketball, baseball, or soccer? Maybe birthdays, graduations, weddings, and funerals? These valued traditions, customs, and artifacts are visible aspects of culture that have shaped American society. While culture is expressed through these avenues, culture—at its core—is much deeper. A culture is a dynamic (Adams & Markus, 2004; Bandura, 2002) "shared system of meanings" (Trompenaars & Hampden-Turner, 1998, p. 13). Through this system, flowing patterns of implicit and explicit meaning are influenced not only by the people who currently comprise the culture but also by the collective generations who came before them (Bandura, 2002; Bellah et al., 2008; Waggoner, 2011). Patterns of meaning are influenced by prior generations, who manifested the culture—as they knew it—in the culture's practices (Adams & Markus, 2004), artifacts (Kroeber & Kluckhohn, 1952, as cited in Adams & Markus, 2004; Schein, 2009, 2010), and institutions (Bellah et al., 2008; Kroeber & Kluckhohn, 1952, as cited in Adams & Markus, 2004; Waggoner, 2011). These aspects of culture are explicit and observable.

But culture is more than just the observable. Culture is comprised of patterns of meaning that shape—and are shaped by—the way we think. Culture shapes the underlying assumptions that guide human thought and behavior (Adams & Markus, 2004). Using these assumptions learned from culture, we evaluate the world around us. With these underlying assumptions, we look through a cultural lens that helps us define and distinguish between: "evil versus good, dirty versus clean, dangerous versus safe, forbidden versus permitted, decent versus indecent, moral versus immoral, ugly versus beautiful, unnatural versus natural, abnormal versus normal, paradoxical versus logical, irrational versus rational" (Hofstede & Hofstede, 2005, p. 8).

Imagine these patterns of meaning flowing between you and the social system (e.g., the organization, your family, or society as a whole). Imagine yourself influencing—and being influenced by—others' underlying assumptions (Adams & Markus, 2004) about what is beautiful, normal, evil, or forbidden.

These underlying assumptions represent implicit aspects of culture, most notably the norms shared amongst people of the culture (Kitayama et al., 2007; Oyserman & Lee, 2008). Culture influences "both the *what* and the *how* of thinking" (Oyserman & Lee, 2008, p. 326).

As an example, think about one or two values that you learned from the family in which you were raised. In your family, *what* was important? Now, consider *how* you learned those values. Did your parents tell you about those values? Did you learn from their example? Did you learn "what not to do" by observing other people—maybe brothers and sisters—whom your parents scolded or discussed as having poor behavior? Did you learn your family's values by being praised for behaviors that aligned with those values or scolded for behaviors that contradicted those values?

Culture influences the content of thinking, i.e., the *what* (Oyserman & Lee, 2008), and the shared system of meanings (Trompenaars & Hampden-Turner, 1998). These patterns of meaning (Adams & Markus, 2004) create a lens through which humans "interpret their experience and guide their action" (Trompenaars & Hampden-Turner, 1998, p. 24). In this way, culture also influences the process of thinking, i.e., the *how* (Oyserman & Lee, 2008). Your lens shares commonalities with the lenses of other people in the same social system. Within this common social environment, culture is collectively learned and perpetuated as you and other people identify your individual roles within the culture (Hofstede & Hofstede, 2005).

Through these flowing patterns of meaning, the social system's (e.g., the organization's) shared meanings and practices influence you and other people within the social system. Similarly, your patterns of meaning and practice also flow toward and influence the social system. Figure 3 shows the Socio-Cultural Learning Model, demonstrating how the individual and the social system (e.g., the organization) influence each other through culture. This bidirectional cultural influence flows between you and the social system, a phenomenon referred to as mutual constitution (Adams & Markus, 2004; Akün et al., 2003; Bandura, 2002; Kitayama et al., 2007).

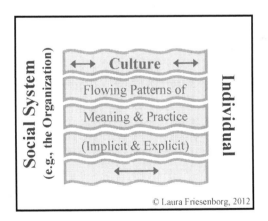

Figure 3. Socio-Cultural Learning Model.

Sources: Adams & Markus, 2004; Kitayama et al., 2007.

Take a look at the Socio-Cognitive Systems Learning Model in Figure 4. You'll see that the cultural flow between the individual and the organization is depicted at the center of the organization's values, learned social behaviors, and outcomes. This is because the cultural patterns of meaning and practice that flow between—and mutually influence—the individual and the social system (e.g., the organization) actually shape the ways that we perceive ourselves, other people, and the environment. Culture influences the things we value and the ways we think and act. As a result, culture influences the outcomes of our interactions with other people. In other words, culture shapes our socio-cognitive processes.

Socio-cognitive processes are defined as "patterns of thinking, feeling, and acting" (Hofstede & Hofstede, 2005, p. 3) relating to human interaction. These patterns are shaped collectively by innate human nature and cultural learning, as well as influenced by individual personality. Socio-cognitive processes may also be referred to as mental programs (Hofstede & Hofstede, 2005), mental models (Senge, 2006a), or theories-in-use (Argyris, 2000; Argyris & Schön, 1996). To build understanding of Argyris' (1998, 2000, 2004, 2006a, 2006b, 2010) theory and its emphasis on social and cognitive skill development, this book refers to such patterns as socio-cognitive processes.

Hofstede and Hofstede (2005) focused their research on the cultural learning element and its influence on patterns of emotion, thought, and behavior. They described the development of these patterns as programmed by an individual's lifetime of experiences. These patterns are heavily influenced by the social systems in which you have interacted most throughout your lifetime. These social systems may include: your immediate family, extended family, school system (including the peers in

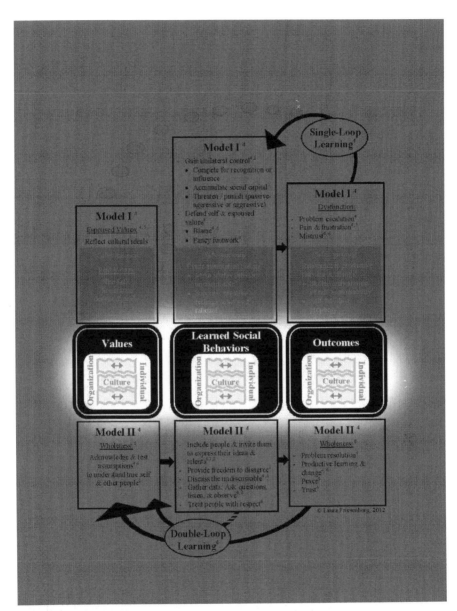

Figure 4. Socio-Cognitive Systems Learning Model:
Highlighting Culture.

Sources: [1] Adams & Markus, 2004; [2] Kitayama et al., 2007; [3] Bandura, 2002;
[4] Argyris, 2000, 2004, 2010; Argyris & Schön, 1996; [5] Schein, 2009; [6] Mezirow,
2003; Palmer, 2004, 2011; [7] Csikszentmihalyi, 2003; [8] Walsh, 2010; [9] Brehm, 2009.

your class, athletic teams, and music groups), neighborhood, network of family friends, online social networks, organizations, and regional, national, and global societies. Each of these social systems has a culture.

In your life, what are some of the social systems for which you feel the strongest affiliation? How have those social systems influenced your values and behaviors?

These social systems influence you by establishing norms for the ways you should think, feel, and act (i.e., your socio-cognitive processes). Similarly, you—as an individual—may influence the norms held by the social system, either by reinforcing the existing norms or by influencing a change in norms (Hofstede & Hofstede, 2005).

Underlying assumptions are at the heart of norms, which determine the ways people should think feel, and act. These underlying assumptions are culturally learned, and they provide the lens through which you see and make sense of the world.

Underlying Assumptions

Deeply held beliefs or underlying assumptions are housed implicitly at the very core of the culture (Conbere & Heorhiadi, 2006; Mezirow, 2003; Trompenaars and Hampden-Turner, 1998). Underlying assumptions reflect your worldview, which is comprised of the foundational frameworks that you use to interpret your experiences and understand reality. As Nord explained, "There is no such thing as uninterpreted experience" (Nord, 1995, as cited in Glanzer, 2011, p. 20). All life experiences are interpreted through the lens of your worldview, contributing to your underlying assumptions. Thus, as worldview is culturally learned, so too are your underlying assumptions (Glanzer, 2011; Waggoner, 2011).

Through socialization (Kitayama et al., 2007), the culture's underlying assumptions are shared (Adams & Markus, 2004; Conbere & Heorhiadi, 2006), influencing your own deeply held beliefs or underlying assumptions (Argyris, 2000; Conbere & Heorhiadi, 2006; Mezirow, 2003). As the cultural patterns flow within the social system, those patterns generate *"dynamic construction* of human psychological experience" (Adams & Markus, 2004, p. 354; authors' emphasis). This is the process of cultural learning (Adams & Markus, 2004). Through this process, the culture imprints its underlying assumptions (Conbere & Heorhiadi, 2006; Mezirow, 2003), which serve as the foundation for your "psychological system for action" (Kitayama et al., 2007, p. 138). These underlying assumptions are based on judgments that you use to make sense of: the environment, rules for thought and behavior (Kitayama et al., 2007), yourself, and other people (Bandura, 2002; Kitayama et al., 2007).

The Environment

Culture influences—and is influenced by—the physical and social environment (Hofstede & Hofstede, 2005; Kitayama et al., 2007). You view the environment through a cultural lens, based on the culture's underlying assumptions. Through this lens, you take stock of the environment around you. The cultures of the social systems, with which you most closely identify, collectively shape your lens. In this way, you see and judge your environment according to how those social systems judge the world, with underlying assumptions that distinguish between aspects that the cultures consider desirable and those they consider undesirable. These underlying assumptions about the environment are intricately interwoven with cultural rules for thought and behavior (Kitayama et al., 2007).

Rules for Thought and Behavior

Within a culture, some behavioral rules are written as policies, procedures, or laws. Even more rules for thought and behavior, though, are unwritten. These are norms that you learn through acculturation, learning that happens as a result of immersion within the culture. Through these norms, you know what the social system expects of you—what is considered "normal." These are cultural parameters for the ways you think and behave.

"Effective participation in human culture typically requires the individual to behave according to a vast set of externally structured, meaningful guidelines, including norms, laws, morals, scripts, traditions, and other rules" (Baumeister, Zang, & Vohs, 2004, p. 113). Such rules are learned through a cyclical two-step process. This process begins with you sensing stimuli, such as language, from the outside world (Aslin & Newport, 2012; Ford, 1999). Second, you make sense of those stimuli by identifying patterns of acceptable behaviors and generalizing those patterns into rules for thought and behavior that may be applied across contexts (Aslin & Newport, 2012; Baumeister et al., 2004; Kolb & Kolb, 2009).

This complex system of rules includes some rules that are spoken and some that are unspoken. As the cultural patterns of meaning flow between you and the other people within the social system (Adams & Markus, 2004), cultural rules influence your deeply held, underlying assumptions. At the same time, your underlying assumptions may influence the culture's written or unwritten rules (Adams & Markus, 2004; Bandura, 2002; Conbere & Heorhiadi, 2006; Kitayama et al., 2007). In this way, cultural rules are either affirmed or changed. This process of cultural influence represents a dynamic interchange between you and the social system (Bandura, 2002; Kolb & Kolb, 2009).

Humans are designed to live culturally (Adams & Markus, 2004; Hofstede & Hofstede, 2005; Kitayama et al., 2007). They have an innate ability to regulate behavior, as well as adapt their behavior to the complex system of social rules (Aslin & Newport, 2012; Hofstede & Hofstede, 2005). However, learning this complex system of social rules is no simple task. Complex social rules are challenging to navigate, particularly as we encounter new social contexts (Baumeister et al., 2004). Human agency is one way to describe how we navigate social rules (Bandura, 2002).

Human agency. Human agency is your ability level to control the circumstances of your life, in order to achieve your desired outcomes. Agency is affected by your deeply held, underlying assumptions that guide your thinking and regulate your behavior (Bandura 2002; Kitayama et al., 2007). Through cultural learning about the rules for thought and behavior, people pursue order and constancy in their environment. This system of behavioral regulation links cultural meaning to human thought and action (Quinn & Holland, 1995), a phenomenon referred to as the cultural mode of being (Kitayama et al., 2007). The cultural mode of being "is an integral part of a larger collective process by which culture is created, preserved, and changed" (Kitayama et al., 2007, p. 139). As a culture's patterns of meaning flow, bidirectional influence occurs between you and the social system, mutually influencing each other (Adams & Markus, 2004; Akün et al., 2003; Bandura, 2002; Kitayama et al., 2007) toward order and constancy (Quinn & Holland, 1995).

Multiple layers of culture. Underlying assumptions are threaded throughout the culture. However, not all individuals within the same national culture will hold identical sets of underlying assumptions. While they tend to have some underlying assumptions in common, variances may occur. This may be due, in part, to influences from multiple layers of culture. In other words, you may more closely affiliate with subcultures or microcultures that may be nested within the national culture, more so than affiliating with the national culture itself. A culture's multiple layers may include: regional, ethnic, religious, or language affiliation; gender; generation; social class; and organization. These layers may—or may not—hold different underlying assumptions from the dominant, national culture. While between-group differences may exist among the layers of culture (Hofstede & Hofstede, 2005; Schein, 2010), within-group differences are also prevalent (Glanzer, 2011).

Commonalities exist among the underlying assumptions of people who share the top layer of culture, the national level. For example, on a macro-level, the American culture has a rule-based structure, espousing that all people should be treated equally according to the rules (Trompenaars & Hampden-Turner, 1998). However, the distinct layers of culture identified by Hofstede and Hofstede (2005) influence the deeply held, underlying assumptions amongst individuals who affiliate with a particular group within that layer of culture. For example, a CEO and an employee in an entry-level position at the same organization likely have different deeply held, underlying assumptions about what "equality" and "following the rules" mean and how effective they are in practice, particularly if the CEO and entry-level employee are members of disparate social classes.

The social rules held by people within the distinct layers of culture may vary (Hofstede & Hofstede, 2005). Furthermore, the dominant culture may target smaller subcultures with distinct social rules. For example, critical theorists argue that people of the wealthy dominant culture maintain their dominant status by imposing social rules that target and oppress the people of less powerful subcultures (Brookfield, 2005; Fromm, 1994). We'll talk more about this in Chapter 6.

Affordances and constraints. Perhaps derived from your social standing and power status within the multiple layers of culture (Brookfield, 2005; Fromm, 1994), "each individual's mode of being is both constantly afforded and constrained by behaviors, expectations, or evaluations of others" (Kitayama et al., 2007, p. 138). This means that the culture has rules—both written and unwritten—about the freedoms that it provides and those it withholds from people.

You interpret those affordances, constraints, expectations, and judgments using your deeply held, underlying assumptions about how people should think and behave (Conbere & Heorhiadi, 2006). These underlying assumptions represent the culture's flowing patterns of meaning, patterns which create rules for thought and behavior through a complex system of shared social norms (Kitayama et al., 2007). Social norms are tightly woven into the culture, serving to maintain order and constancy within the culture. Order and constancy (Fromm, 1994; Quinn & Holland, 1995) are further reinforced through the culture's artifacts and institutions (Kroeber & Kluckhohn, 1952, in Adams & Markus, 2004; Trompenaars & Hampden-Turner, 1998; Waggoner, 2011).

Such institutions include organizations. People are attracted to organizations that have clear, familiar identities, rather than organizations whose identities are more ambiguous. We seek organizations that have the same framework of prescribed behavioral rules to which we are accustomed. In seeking familiar social rules, we tend to gravitate toward organizations with values that are homogeneous to our own. In this way, we are folded into the fabric of the organization's homogeneity (Bryant, 2011).

Underlying assumptions about the environment and rules for thought and behavior are intricately intertwined with underlying assumptions about yourself and other people. For example, a culture's flowing patterns of meaning about beauty and the desirability of such beauty may influence your self-concept, the way you judge others, the underlying assumptions that regulate clothing choices, and perhaps the environments where you choose to insert yourself. Your deeply held, underlying assumptions are related to the cultural environment and its rules about thought and behavior, which you project onto yourself and other people (Bandura, 2002; Conbere & Heorhiadi, 2006; Kitayama et al., 2007).

The Self

Deeply held beliefs are generally learned subconsciously, beginning in early childhood (Conbere & Heorhiadi, 2006). You affiliate with certain groups (Oyserman & Lee, 2008) at various layers of culture, such as national culture; regional, ethnic, religious, or language affiliation; gender; generation; social class; or organization (Hofstede & Hofstede, 2005). This affiliation is based upon how closely you identify with the social group (Hofstede & Hofstede, 2005; Oyserman & Lee, 2008). In this way, culture shapes your social identity (Oyserman & Lee, 2008).

Self-evaluation. Through affiliation with social groups amongst the layers of culture, you evaluate yourself, based upon the assumptions you learned from the cultural groups with which you identify. This self-evaluation is based on the affiliate culture's assessment of individuals' desirability. You compare yourself and other people with culturally derived meanings about what is beautiful, what is normal, and what is good (Hofstede & Hofstede, 2005). Self-concept is related to your perceptions of how closely your own attributes match what the culture defines as desirable (Hofstede & Hofstede, 2005; Kitayama et al., 2007).

In addition to self-evaluation of personal traits, you evaluate your thoughts and behavior according to the cultural norms which dictate rules for thought and behavior. You compare your thoughts and behaviors with the culturally derived standards for what is considered "forbidden versus permitted" (Hofstede & Hofstede, 2005, p. 8). In this way, you assess whether thoughts and behaviors are "dangerous versus safe, ...decent versus indecent, moral versus immoral, ...abnormal versus normal, paradoxical versus logical, irrational versus rational" (Hofstede & Hofstede, 2005, p. 8).

Locus of control. Your perceptions surrounding thought and behavior, particularly as they relate to yourself, may be skewed. Underlying assumptions about the causality of circumstances are influenced by locus of control. In the American culture, when bad things happen to us, we tend to attribute those negative circumstances to external factors. When something bad happens to us, we maintain that it's not our fault. In contrast, when bad things happen to *other* people, we tend to blame them for the misfortune they are experiencing (Csikszentmihalyi, 2003).

Human agency. Through the American culture's lens of individualism (Bandura, 2002; Bellah et al., 2008; Kitayama et al., 2007; Oyserman & Lee, 2008; Waggoner, 2011), the modes of human agency are culturally learned. People use these modes of agency in the attempt to influence what happens to them and take charge of their own destiny. Bandura identified three modes of human agency in his Social Cognitive Theory: (a) individual agency, (b) proxy agency, and (c) collective agency. We use all three modes, at one time or another, as we seek to control the circumstances of our lives.

Individual agency relates to the underlying assumptions you have about yourself, while proxy and collective agencies relate to the underlying assumptions you have about other people and their relationship to you. All three modes of agency are significantly influenced by self-efficacy, your confidence in your ability to control your own destiny. This confidence shapes your patterns of emotion, thought, and behavior, as well as what motivates you (Bandura, 2002, p. 270).

In the individualistic, American culture (Bandura, 2002; Bellah et al., 2008; Kitayama et al., 2007; Oyserman & Lee, 2008; Waggoner, 2011), Bandura (2002) found that managers achieved the highest degrees of both self-efficacy and work productivity when they employed individual agency. With individual agency, people believe that—through their own means—they can influence what happens. Bandura found that, through individual agency, managers crafted their actions in a strategic attempt to control their own circumstances.

Despite this finding for the overall culture, within-culture differences were also evident. Individualism manifests differently in different regions of the U.S. In addition, while the American culture is predominantly individualistic, people within the culture have varying degrees of individualism and collectivism. People employ all three modes of agency, although they tend to exhibit preferred modes depending on the context. For example, people may employ individual agency at work, yet employ collective agency with their families (Bandura, 2002).

Other People

Your underlying assumptions about other people reflect your assumptions about their personal attributes, thoughts, and behaviors, within the framework of cultural norms. In this way, the culture influences your underlying assumptions about other people. In individualistic cultures, such as the American culture, we evaluate others in terms of how we can benefit from their capacity to better our own circumstances. Specifically, we consider how they can help us achieve our own desired results through (a) proxy or (b) collective agency (Bandura, 2002).

With proxy agency, we have deeply held, underlying assumptions about how we can capitalize on the resources, expertise, power, or influence of other people. We believe that by aligning with more powerful people, we will enjoy power by proxy (Bandura, 2002). This is related to the assumption that people may increase their own social capital by associating with others who are recognized for their social influence or positional power (Adler & Kwon, 2002; Belliveau, O'Reilly, & Wade, 1996). Proxy stems from association, by strategically positioning oneself with powerful people (Bandura, 2002).

Different from proxy agency, collective agency is the capacity to control our own circumstances through a collective effort. In the collectivist culture of Hong Kong (Bandura, 2002; Kitayama et al., 2007; Oyserman & Lee, 2008), managers achieved the highest degrees of self-efficacy and work productivity when they employed collective agency, focusing on group work and group achievement.

Like all modes of agency, collective agency is thought to be present—in some form—in virtually all cultures. While the dominant American culture has strong tendencies toward individualism, Americans are predicted to practice collective agency to some degree in some contexts (Bandura, 2002; Trompenaars & Hampden-Turner, 1998). In addition, due to within-group differences (Glanzer, 2011), some individuals within the American culture may have a natural orientation toward collectivism, more so than individualism. Subsequently, Bandura (2002) found that Americans with a collectivist orientation achieved higher degrees of self-efficacy and work productivity through group-based work, rather than individual-based work. Even though collectivism is secondary to individualism in the United States (Trompenaars & Hampden-Turner, 1998), some people do have a personal preference for collectivism (Bandura, 2002).

Connection to Social Cognition

Your own socio-cognitive patterns of values, behaviors, and outcomes mix with the socio-cognitive patterns of the social system (Adams & Markus, 2004; Bandura, 2002; Kitayama et al., 2007) as they flow culturally between you (Adams & Markus, 2004). Understanding the role of acculturation is essential for understanding your own underlying assumptions (Conbere & Heorhiadi, 2006; Oyserman & Lee, 2008).

Values, learned social behaviors, and outcomes— together—create a cognitive process that guides social interaction. The bidirectional, cultural interchange between the underlying assumptions of the individual and the social system (Adams & Markus, 2004; Bandura, 2002; Kitayama et al., 2007) influences each element of the socio-cognitive process.

While Argyris' research does not specifically examine the bidirectional influence between culture and an individual's underlying assumptions (Argyris, 2000, 2004), he and Schön did elude to the role of cultural learning. They stated, "Individuals are programmed with Model I theories-in-use" (Argyris & Schön, 1996,

p. 106). This is an important point. With this statement, Argyris and Schön described the dysfunctional Model I system as being culturally programmed. Through this process, Model I dysfunctions are fueled and perpetuated by the culture of many social systems, including American society.

4

Model I
Socio-Cognitive Process:
The Cultural Default

The Model I process is a dysfunctional thought-behavior pattern identified by Argyris and his colleague Schön (1996). This thought-behavior pattern is driven by self-centered desires and goals (Kitayama et al., 2007)—as well as untested, underlying assumptions (Argyris, 2000)—which shape Model I values, learned social behaviors, and outcomes.

If Model I thought-behavior patterns are so dysfunctional, why do people adopt these patterns? Model I patterns are learned through acculturation, by being immersed in a culture—such as the American culture—which practices Model I (Argyris & Schön, 1996). In Chapter 3, we discussed the Socio-Cultural Learning Model, which shows how cultural patterns of meaning and practice flowing between the individual and the social system. The Model I process is learned through this process.

Beginning from a young age (Conbere & Heorhiadi, 2006; Hofstede & Hofstede, 2005), cognitive processes—or the ways we think—are primed by culture (Oyserman & Lee, 2008). Model I is the American cultural "default" process for social cognition (Argyris & Schön, 1996; Edmondson, 1996). This suggests that the Model I process is subconsciously learned through acculturation, rather than consciously learned (Argyris & Schön, 1996). Argyris' (2000, 2004) research on organization learning found that Model I thought-behavior patterns are pervasive in the cultures of U.S. organizations.

Model I: Values

The Model I socio-cognitive process includes thought-behavior patterns characterized by a dance of deception and contradiction (Argyris, 2000, 2004; Palmer, 2011). Such a dance is evident not only in social interaction between ourselves and other people but also internally within ourselves (Palmer, 2004), through the contradiction between our real values and the values that we espouse. This means that the words we say—the values we claim to have—often contradict our deeply held values, which are reflected in our actions (Argyris, 2010; Conbere & Heorhiadi, 2006; Palmer, 2011; Schein, 2009).

For example, a business executive might describe his children as his top priority, yet he works 80 hours—and seven days—per week, leaving limited time for his family. As another example, organization leaders might say that they value employees, yet the organization might operate a cutthroat environment where employees are expendable. In these examples, the values that people claim are different than the real values that their actions reflect.

We learn values from others in the social systems to which we belong. We also learn the elaborate system of social norms designed to perpetuate those values by observing the behaviors modeled by others in the social system (Hofstede & Hofstede, 2005). In cultures where the Model I socio-cognitive process is prevalent, we also learn the intricate dance between real values and espoused values (Argyris, 2000, 2004, 2006b; Conbere & Heorhiadi, 2006).

Figure 5 shows the relationship between Model I values and the social behaviors and outcomes that are shaped by those values. The Model I socio-cognitive process is a cycle of dysfunction.

Real Values

In the dominant American culture, which is highly individualistic, our real values reflect cultural individualism (Bellah et al., 2008; Kitayama et al., 2007; Waggoner, 2011). "...The worth of the individual self [is] fundamental to the ethos of the American way of life" (Waggoner, 2011, p. 7).

Contradictory to the idealistic values that we espouse, or claim to have, our primary real value is the self. In order to live within this contradiction, our self-centered values are often held subconsciously, under the veil of espoused values that reflect cultural ideals. To serve the self, we value people and things that advance our own desires and goals (Bandura, 2002; Bellah et al., 2008; Conbere & Heorhiadi, 2006; Kitayama et al., 2007). People's hearts are gripped by their egocentric values: their self-centered desires and goals (Bellah et al., 2008). These values may produce greed and an "indifference to the suffering of others" (Palmer, 2004, p. 1).

The individualism of the American culture influences the value of self. Evidence of individualistic values can be found on

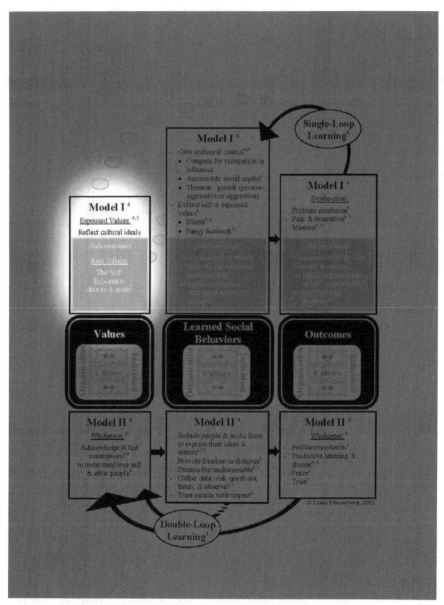

Figure 5. Socio-Cognitive Systems Learning Model: Highlighting Model I Values.

Sources: [1] Adams & Markus, 2004; [2] Kitayama et al., 2007; [3] Bandura, 2002; [4] Argyris, 2000, 2004, 2010; Argyris & Schön, 1996; [5] Schein, 2009; [6] Mezirow, 2003; Palmer, 2004, 2011; [7] Csikszentmihalyi, 2003; [8] Walsh, 2010; [9] Brehm, 2009.

Facebook, Twitter, Instagram, and other social media. These media are designed for individuals to post personal anecdotes, under the premise that their social networks are interested in their personal thoughts and experiences. The widespread use of social media has strengthened the trend toward "hyperindividualism" (Waggoner, 2011, p. 14).

How would a social system effectively operate if cultural norms promoted the open admission that each person's primary value was the self? What would our social system look like if people abandoned their espoused values—their cultural ideals— and, instead, even more openly touted their self-centered desires and goals for power and pleasure? With people openly seeking to serve only themselves, how would they find common ground? How would people be able to come together, working together to benefit the greater good? Would members of the social system have the capacity to uphold a common set of social rules for thought and behavior, or would there be anarchy?

Perhaps as a built-in mechanism to provide order and avoid social chaos (Quinn & Holland, 1995), the Model I socio-cognitive process is marked by espoused values that reflect shared cultural ideals, which cloak—or hide—our real, egocentric values (Argyris, 2000, 2004, 2006b; Kitayama et al., 2007; Schein, 2009).

Espoused Values

Through the Model I socio-cognitive process (Argyris, 2000, 2004, 2006b), our real values are centered on our own desires and goals (Kitayama et al., 2007). These desires and goals may be hidden in the subconscious (Hofstede & Hofstede, 2005), shrouded by politically correct, espoused values (Schein, 2009).

Our espoused values reflect cultural ideals (Kitayama et al., 2007), which are expressed by the cultures with which we most closely identify. These are called espoused values because we claim them as true—and often we even believe them to be true—although our behaviors do not necessarily align with the values we are espousing (Argyris, 2000, 2004, 2010; Conbere & Heorhiadi, 2006; Schein, 2009). With the Model I socio-cognitive process, our espoused values and our behaviors often conflict (Argyris, 2000, 2004, 2010; Conbere & Heorhiadi, 2006), yet we are skillfully unaware of this contradiction (Argyris, 2000; Conbere & Heorhiadi, 2006; Palmer, 2011).

The cultural ideals (Kitayama et al., 2007) that we espouse as values (Schein, 2009) often do not reflect our real, egocentric values (Conbere & Heorhiadi, 2006; Kitayama et al., 2007), so it is no wonder that we have false underlying assumptions about each other. Referred to as pluralistic ignorance (Adams & Markus, 2004), our false underlying assumptions about other people's beliefs and values stem from our failure to test those assumptions for validity. Instead, our assumptions about other people's beliefs and values remain mere assumptions, yet we consider them to be truths (Argyris, 2000, 2004, 2006b, 2010; Palmer, 2011).

"In interpreting people's statements about their values, it is important to distinguish between the *desirable* and the *desired*: how people think the world ought to be versus what people want for themselves" (Hofstede & Hofstede, 2005, p. 21, authors' emphasis). While *our* real values revolve around our own desires and goals (i.e., "the desired"), we expect *others'* real values to align with the ideology of their espoused values (i.e., "the desirable"). This means that, though our own words contradict our own actions, we expect other people's words and actions to align. As a result, a paradox exists between our own values and our expectations regarding other people's values (Hofstede & Hofstede, 2005).

For example, we expect others to be open and honest and to have integrity. Yet, these are espoused values that may contradict our own Model I behaviors, which are driven by real values (Argyris, 2010). Model I's real values are centered on individualistic desires and goals (Kitayama et al., 2007), not idealistic espoused values, such as openness, honesty, and integrity.

Empowerment (Argyris, 1998; Ford, 1999) and employee engagement are also examples of this paradox (Hofstede & Hofstede, 2005). Empowerment (Argyris, 1998; Ford, 1999) and employee engagement are commonly held, misguided substitutes for organization learning. These are often espoused values that shroud management's real values (Conbere & Heorhiadi, 2006; Schein, 2009) of power and control (Argyris, 1998; Brookfield, 2000, 2005; Fromm, 1994).

Empowerment values. The American culture espouses values related to "empowering individual expression" (Waggoner, 2011, p. 7). In fact, the First Amendment of the United States Constitution empowers the guarantee of free speech (United States Congress, 1789), a value that is highly espoused by the culture. However, while this value is claimed, it is not always real. Such individual expression is welcome if it supports the espoused values of the dominant culture, but oppressive criticism or hostility may result if the individual's message contradicts the dominant culture's espoused values (Conbere & Heorhiadi, 2006; Waggoner, 2011).

In an article entitled "Empowerment: The Emperor's New Clothes," Argyris (1998) exposed the disparity between organizations' espoused values about empowerment versus their real values. Typical organizations in the dominant American culture espouse the value of empowerment, but their behaviors contradict those claims, suggesting disparate real values hiding beneath the cloak of espoused empowerment. Argyris wrote, "The change programs and practices we employ are full of inner contradictions that cripple innovation, motivation, and drive. At the same time, CEOs subtly undermine empowerment. Managers love empowerment in theory, but the command-and-control model is what they trust and know best" (p. 98).

While managers exhibit "skilled unawareness" of this contradiction, mixed messages make the contradiction glaringly obvious to employees. Employees are cynical of managers' claims to empower them (Ford, 1999), which may lead to mistrust. The disparity between espoused and real values is not limited to managers. Employees also demonstrate a contradiction between espoused and real values related to the issue of empowerment. Employees espouse the value of empowerment, yet they may avoid real opportunities for empowerment when those opportunities also require accountability. Both managers and employees likely have mixed feelings about the issue of empowerment (Argyris, 1998).

Employee engagement values. Yesterday's empowerment initiatives have been repackaged and are sold as today's employee engagement initiatives. Employee engagement initiatives, while well-meaning, are often merely recycled versions of employee empowerment programs (Argyris, 1998). Employee engagement has been widely studied (Kimball, 2011). In the bulk of the literature, the process for achieving employee engagement reads like a series of prescriptive items on a check-off list (Argyris, 2010). Such items might include: identifying engagement drivers specific to the organization, creating a culture that recognizes engaged employees, fostering diversity and inclusion, and building employee trust in the organization's leaders ("Ten Ways to Maximize Employee Engagement," 2009). However, do these items on the check-off list reflect the organization's real values? Or do these strategies simply reflect espoused values? Might employee engagement, in itself, be an espoused value?

Employee engagement has largely been explored conceptually, rather than through empirical research. Few studies have examined the role of conversation as it relates to employee engagement (Ford, 1999; Kimball, 2011; van der Merwe, Chermack, Kulikowich, & Yang, 2007). Of the existing, empirically based literature, employee engagement tends to be measured using self-reported, quantitative surveys as the sole source of data. This research design poses a validity problem. The problem is that questionnaires measure espoused values, not real values (Schein, 2009).

When only quantitative data are used, the culture can be studied only superficially (Argyris, 2010; Schein, 2009) because quantitative questionnaires cannot measure the deeply held, underlying assumptions that "define the essence of cultures" (Schein, 2009, p. 206). Furthermore, "the *patterning* of cultural assumptions into a paradigm cannot be revealed by a questionnaire" (p. 206, author's emphasis). As a result, the quantitative questionnaire may be "neither reliable nor valid, because to validate formal measures of something as deep and complex as cultural assumptions is intrinsically very difficult" (p. 206). Statistical validity is incapable of untangling espoused values from real values (Argyris, 2006b; Schein, 2009).

Values Contradiction: Real versus Espoused Values

Why do we espouse the values idealized by the dominant culture, rather than claiming our *real* values? Disguising real values—covering them with a cloak of espoused values (Palmer,

2004; Schein, 2009)—is culturally learned. This process was learned so early in life that we take it for granted (Argyris, 2006b; Hofstede & Hofstede, 2005; Mezirow, 2003).

Espoused values typically stem from the ideals of people in power. People who do not hold power within a culture may adopt the espoused values of those in power (Kitayama et al., 2007). If individuals realize their deeply held, underlying assumptions and behaviors contrast with the values of those in power within the dominant culture, they may experience frustration or anxiety (Bryant, 2011; Conbere & Heorhiadi, 2006). Perhaps individuals adopt the espoused values of the dominant culture as a method to avoid dissonance between themselves and those in power (Conbere & Heorhiadi, 2006; Kitayama et al., 2007).

With widespread acculturation of deeply held, underlying assumptions and general agreement about espoused values, what is so problematic about the Model I socio-cognitive process? "Because they were acquired so early in our lives, many values remain unconscious to those who hold them. Therefore they cannot be discussed, nor can they be directly observed by outsiders. They can only be inferred from the way people act..." (Hofstede & Hofstede, 2005, p. 10). While the culture generally agrees on its espoused values, conflict arises when people's behaviors contradict the values they espouse. Rather than reflecting the values we claim, our behaviors reflect our real values, which may be held in the subconscious (Hofstede & Hofstede, 2005). The contradiction between real and espoused values is problematic, as evidenced by the behaviors that are prevalent in the Model I socio-cognitive process (Argyris, 2000, 2004, 2006b, 2010; Conbere & Heorhiadi, 2006).

Model I: Learned Social Behaviors

The Model I socio-cognitive process makes the mistake of using instrumental learning strategies, rather than communicative learning strategies, for social interaction. Instrumental learning and communicative learning are two different approaches to learning. They constitute the "two major domains of learning, each having its own purpose, logic of inquiry, criteria of rationality, and mode of validating beliefs" (Habermas, 1984, as cited in Mezirow, 2000, p. 8).

Instrumental learning is a controlled, systematic process for learning new tasks or procedures. It is designed to fix a problem by controlling either the elements perceived as causing the problem or the elements perceived as providing the solution (Bullard, 2011; Gudynas, 2011; Walsh, 2010). The instrumental learning approach is suitable for object-related tasks, as opposed to people-oriented tasks. As a result, instrumental learning is appropriate for tasks such as accounting, computer programming, and operating machinery.

In contrast, communicative learning is designed for developing common understanding among people. Learning through dialogue with other people is essential for building relationships and solving interpersonal problems (see Table 1). While instrumental learning changes *what* we know, communicative learning changes *how* we know (Mezirow, 2000, 2003).

In Western cultures, instrumental learning is the predominant approach for learning. The problem is that instrumental learning is applied not only to object-related tasks but also to people-related contexts, such as management, for which instrumental learning is not well-suited. For people-related contexts, communicative learning is the appropriate approach. Seeking to control people is generally not the most effective approach for eliciting productivity and innovation (Gudynas, 2011; Habermas, 1984, as cited in Mezirow, 2000; Mezirow, 2000, 2003; Walsh, 2010).

Table 1

Differences between Instrumental and Communicative Learning

Characteristics	Instrumental learning	Communicative learning
Goal	Task performance	Shared understanding
Method	Instruction	Dialogue
Interpersonal approach	Control and influence others	Listen and learn the meaning of others' words
Commitment	External	Internal
Utility	Technical and emotionally neutral procedures	Collaboration and resolution of relationship problems

Sources: Argyris, 1998; Brookfield, 2005; Habermas, 1984, as cited in Mezirow, 2000; Mezirow, 2000, 2003.

"Already too much human imagination is channeled into 'solving' problems the wrong way. What we lack is the imagination to think about how to live differently, how to unravel the power structures that obstruct change, and how to rethink 'development'" (Bullard, 2011, p. 142). The Model I socio-cognitive process and, in particular, the cultural approach for applying instrumental learning to people-related contexts in organization management, is one such power structure that obstructs change. Productive change cannot occur when we consider another person as a "problem to be solved" or someone that "needs to be controlled." These are characteristics of instrumental learning. We need a new way of thinking—through the communicative learning approach—if we are to effectively lead change (Habermas, 1984, as cited in Mezirow, 2000; Mezirow, 2000, 2003).

Figure 6 shows the relationship between Model I behaviors and how these behaviors relate with Model I values and outcomes. This diagram shows how Model I is perpetuated through a vicious cycle of single-loop learning.

Unilateral Control

In the American culture, most businesses approach organization learning much the same way they approach instrumental learning (Argyris, 2004; Argyris & Schön, 1996; Mezirow, 2000, 2003). Dominant voices emphasize control and influence in order to generate external commitment (Mezirow, 2000, 2003; Palmer, 2004; Walsh, 2010) through strategies such as empowerment or employee engagement (Argyris, 1998; Ford, 1999; Kimball, 2011; van der Merwe et al., 2007). In this way, instrumental learning supports the dysfunctional Model I socio-cognitive process (Argyris, 2000, 2004, 2006b). When people apply instrumental learning to object-oriented tasks, such as accounting, computer programming, or engineering, they tend to test their assumptions throughout the process. However, when businesses approach organization learning and social interaction by applying instrumental learning techniques, they fail to test their underlying assumptions (Argyris, 2006b; Habermas, 1984, as cited in Mezirow, 2000; Mezirow, 2000, 2003).

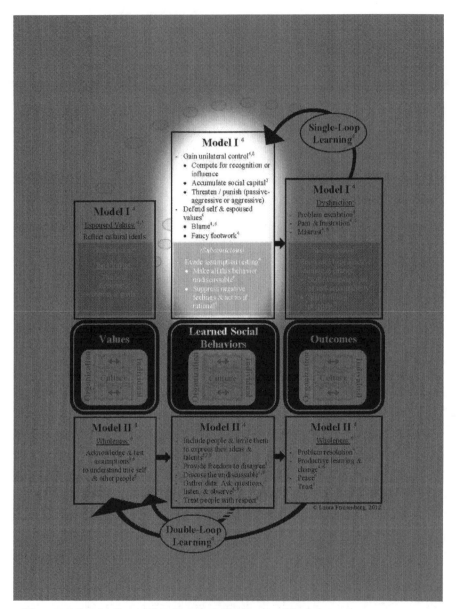

Figure 6. Socio-Cognitive Systems Learning Model:
Highlighting Model I Learned Social Behaviors.

Sources: [1] Adams & Markus, 2004; [2] Kitayama et al., 2007; [3] Bandura, 2002;
[4] Argyris, 2000, 2004, 2010; Argyris & Schön, 1996; [5] Schein, 2009; [6] Mezirow,
2003; Palmer, 2004, 2011; [7] Csikszentmihalyi, 2003; [8] Walsh, 2010; [9] Brehm, 2009.

Prescribed practices. Corporate America develops organization learning processes just as it approaches instrumental-type strategies, by researching best practices. Businesses pinpoint other companies recognized as "learning organizations" and obtain their prescribed list of best practices that, if followed, are presumed to result in organization learning. The business then attempts to replicate that prescription and uses metrics to measure its success in adopting it (Argyris, 2006b, 2010; Argyris & Schön, 1996; Palmer, 2004). While metrics are used to assess the organization's success at prescriptive practices, the validity of the prescriptive practices remains largely untested (Argyris, 2006b, 2010).

Argyris (1998, 2000, 2004, 2006b, 2010) disagreed that prescriptive best practices, orchestrated and controlled by management, are effective in producing organization learning and change. An organization is a unique social system with complex, underlying cultural norms and behavior patterns. Simply covering the organization with a prescribed "learning organization" dressing does not change the organization's untested, underlying assumptions, which guide all interaction within the social system.

Prescriptive practices are based on instrumental learning (Argyris, 2010; Mezirow, 2000, 2003). Prescribed practices such as empowerment and employee engagement use culturally learned social strategies that reflect espoused values. Empowerment and employee engagement would be admirable qualities within an organization, if the organization's real values supported these qualities. The problem is that organizations' real, underlying values typically seek to control people and their circumstances (Argyris, 1998, 2000, 2004, 2010; Bandura, 2002; Ford, 1999; Palmer 2004).

When organizations seek unilateral control, the best they should expect is external commitment—or compliance—from employees. For example, external motivation strategies, such as promotions and monetary bonuses, do appeal to employees' real values of individualistic desires and goals (Kitayama et al., 2007). These external motivation strategies produce only external commitment, though, not the outcome of internal commitment that managers typically expect (Argyris, 1998, 2010; Bandura, 2002).

Empowerment and employee engagement behaviors. People's behaviors are geared toward realizing their real values, not the values they espouse or claim to have. Their real values are based on deeply held assumptions that are individualistic and self-serving. The ego thrives on power and status. Furthermore, a manager's egocentric desires and goals may be threatened by change. This threat may be based on a number of things, such as fear of the potential for losing power or fear of embarrassment if the change efforts are unsuccessful. As a result, the manager may subconsciously avoid—or even obstruct—change efforts (Argyris, 2000, 2004, 2006b, 2010; Conbere & Heorhiadi, 2006; Kitayama et al., 2007).

True organization learning exposes the organization to change (Argyris, 2004; Billett, 2001; Ford, 1999; Kimball, 2011). The potential for learning and change competes with the stability-seeking mechanisms of the organization culture (Hofstede & Hofstede, 2005). While managers may espouse learning and change, their behaviors are control-seeking. Unilateral control is a hallmark, anti-learning strategy that is designed to perpetuate the Model I socio-cognitive process within the organization (Argyris, 1998, 2000).

In reaction to managers' pursuit of unilateral control, employees resist being controlled. They seek to control their own circumstances. Rather than bend to the demands of a control-hungry manager, employees may seek control by expending only minimal effort or by disengaging completely.

This is a social game, with managers and employees each seeking unilateral control, while simultaneously resisting others' efforts to exert control over them. Employees and managers recognize each other's roles in the social game (Hofstede & Hofstede, 2005), which is marked by idealistic values and rife with contradictory behaviors (Argyris, 1998, 2000, 2004; Csikszentmihalyi, 2003; Conbere & Heorhiadi, 2006). Yet, they are blind (Argyris, 1998, 2000, 2004; Carlson, 2013; Conbere & Heorhiadi, 2006) to their own role in the social game (Hofstede & Hofstede, 2005).

Managers espouse that they want to empower employees (Argyris, 1998), yet they shut employees out of decision-making. Efforts for employee engagement are attempts to use incentives and rewards, with the expectation that these external motivators will produce *internal* motivation among employees. Through this process, managers attempt to use their individual agency to try to produce collective agency among employees. However, managers intend to retain individual agency, with no plans to join employees in a true collective focus. Collective agency will not be successful unless employees consider managers to be sincere and trustworthy, when managers include employees in decision-making and work collectively with them (Argyris, 1998; Bandura, 2002; Ford, 1999).

Employees in organizations with command-and-control cultures are not fooled (Argyris, 1998; Csikszentmihalyi, 2003; Ford, 1999). They recognize when employee engagement campaigns merely *espouse* an interest in creating an organization culture that engages employees. People in power within command-and-control cultures have no intention of changing the culture to share power with employees. They do not intend to create a culture that embraces collective decision-making and collective work toward identifying and achieving organization goals.

Employees realize that, regardless of the level of effort they invest, they have little to no voice in the Model I organization and will not be granted opportunity to play a valuable role in bettering the organization (Argyris, 1998; Bandura, 2002; Csikszentmihalyi, 2003). As a result, employees in command-and-control cultures tend to dissociate their personal identities from their roles at work. That is why employee engagement efforts will not work, as long as the talk about co-creating an organization culture built upon collective efforts among managers and employees is only espoused and not real (Argyris, 1998). Employees will not acquire self-efficacy in this way (Bandura, 2002).

While managers' skilled unawareness prevents them from seeing that empowerment (Argyris, 1998; Ford, 1999) and employee engagement are merely espoused values (Schein, 2009) sabotaged by anti-learning tactics (Argyris, 1998, 2000, 2004), employees are not fooled (Csikszentmihalyi, 2003). In response to this social game (Hofstede & Hofstede, 2005) masked as an organization learning strategy (Argyris, 2006a), employees generally make one of two choices. They may disengage (Csikszentmihalyi, 2003; Palmer, 2004), or they may develop strategies for career advancement (Adler & Kwon, 2002), to fulfill their individualistic desires and goals (Kitayama et al., 2007) to join the power elite (Argyris, 2000, 2004).

Management is not the only party operating under the Model I socio-cognitive process. Employees are too. The choice to disengage and the choice to implement tactics to achieve power through management status are both learned social strategies, characteristic of Model I (Argyris, 2000).

Disengagement. "...If management views workers not as valuable, unique individuals but as tools to be discarded when no longer needed, then employees will also regard the firm as nothing more than a machine for issuing paychecks, with no other value or meaning. Under such conditions it is difficult to do a good job, let alone to enjoy one's work. But as Lincoln said, most people cannot be fooled for long, and few people will keep investing their psychic energy into an organization that despises them" (Csikszentmihalyi, 2003, p. 101).

Americans spend the majority of their waking hours at work. Their careers may provide more than just an income. Careers may also provide them with a sense of identity (Bandura, 2002). However, if employees find the work to be demeaning—being relegated to merely follow orders (Argyris, 1998)—they may disengage (Csikszentmihalyi, 2003; Palmer, 2004). Because the demeaning work serves as a reminder of the "painful gap between who [they] truly are and the role [they] play in the so-called real world" (Palmer, 2004, p. 15), employees in command-and-control organization cultures tend to separate one's personal identity from the work role.

Without trust in their leadership and confidence that they can accomplish the desired changes through collective effort (Bandura, 2002), employees tend to avoid participating in the organization's prescribed strategies. They will go through the motions to collect a paycheck, but they will not fully dedicate themselves to the goals of the organization. Employees guard themselves from fully investing in the organization because they perceive their work—and their humanity—as undervalued by management. Employees do not believe they have a valued role in the collective effort to identify and work toward achieving the organization's goals for change. In fact, there may be no collective effort at all. In the case of most Model I organizations, managers identify goals and prescribe the steps to achieve them. The employee is cast from all decision-making processes and has no role except to follow orders (Argyris, 1998). As a result, employees do not have confidence that they can—through collective effort—improve the future of the organization or better their own future, for that matter (Bandura, 2002). This, in turn, leads employees to disengage (Csikszentmihalyi, 2003; Palmer, 2004).

In this type of organization culture (i.e., a Model I culture), any espoused efforts on the part of managers to engage or empower employees will be futile (Argyris, 1998). Employees see this effort for what it really is: a social game (Hofstede & Hofstede, 2005), masking itself as a bona fide initiative to achieve management's espoused values related to collective learning on an organization level (Argyris, 2006a).

Strategies for joining the power elite. Have you ever heard the saying, "If you can't beat 'em, join 'em?" While some employees may respond to the social game of Model I (Argyris, 1998; Hofstede & Hofstede, 2005) by disengaging (Csikszentmihalyi, 2003; Palmer, 2004), others may strategize how to join the power elite. They may strive toward management status in order to enjoy the same power and control that they observe among managers (Argyris, 2000; Palmer, 2004). Managers may exert power (Brookfield, 2005) by capitalizing on the desire among employees to rise to management status. Taking advantage of employees' goals for career advancement, management may create an organization culture that requires long hours and a frenzied pace to achieve recognition, advancement, or simply to stay ahead of the immense workload (Palmer, 2004).

"...Societies often succeed in developing systems of meaning that rationalize and justify even the hardest labor. A saying from the Middle Ages ran: 'Peeling potatoes is as important as building cathedrals, if done for the greater glory of God'" (Csikszentmihalyi, 2003, p. 96). This rationalization and justification of "hard labor" is still prevalent today and is particularly evident in the American culture (Palmer, 2004).

Using the Model I socio-cognitive process (Argyris, 2000, 2004, 2006b), management may "dangle the carrot" of career advancement by appealing to employees' real values—their individualistic desires and goals (Kitayama et al., 2007)—with the stipulation that such advancement requires long hours and a frenzied pace (Palmer, 2004). Such expectations are embedded into both the dominant culture of corporate America and the deeply held, underlying assumptions of many corporate employees seeking career advancement (Adler & Kwon, 2002; Conbere & Heorhiadi, 2006; Palmer, 2004). In this way, the culture appeals to the value of individualistic desires and goals (Kitayama et al., 2007), whereby reinforcing the learned strategy for seeking unilateral control (Argyris, 2000).

In response, employees may develop an obsession to succeed, which may manifest as workaholism. In the process, they "lose touch with [their] souls and disappear into [their] roles" (Palmer, 2004, p. 15). This form of dividedness negatively impacts their families and others around them. In addition, their contributions to those they serve also suffer as the workaholism takes a toll on the health of one's inner self and on the health of the individual's close relationships (Palmer, 2004).

Social Capital

Culture also reinforces the learned social strategy of striving to accumulate social capital (Kitayama et al., 2007). Social capital is defined as "an individual's personal network and elite institutional affiliations" (Belliveau et al., 1996, p. 1572). This means that we try to build power for ourselves by associating with people who have power and influence. Accumulation of social capital (Adler & Kwon, 2002; Belliveau et al., 1996) is a learned social strategy that is characteristic of the Model I socio-cognitive process (Argyris, 2000).

The individual values relationships with others based on the value of their social capital. "Social others are important...only to the extent that they are seen as instrumental in achieving one's own goals and desires" (Kitayama et al., 2007, p. 143). Model I social systems are comprised of individuals competing against each other (Adler & Kwon, 2002; Palmer, 2004), each striving to achieve their own desires and goals (Kitayama et al., 2007), each striving to win (Argyris, 2000). Carlson and Apple (as cited in Glanzer, 2011) explained, "...We are not necessarily playing on a level field in terms of whose voices circulate more widely, whose voices are heard, and whose voices dominate. This is a knotty problem that cannot be wished away" (p. 31).

People are motivated to build social capital in order to increase their proxy agency. By aligning ourselves with beautiful, wealthy, or otherwise desirable people, we increase our capacity to control the circumstances of our own lives. This proxy agency allows us to capitalize on others' expertise, attention, influence, or resources (Bandura, 2002). We benefit from proxy agency through increased social influence (Adler & Kwon, 2002; Belliveau et al., 1996) and sometimes even financial compensation, resulting from plum opportunities offered to us by people who have power and influence (Belliveau et al., 1996).

While proxy agency is not inherently bad (Bandura, 2002), focusing on building social capital (Adler & Kwon, 2002; Belliveau et al., 1996) may distract us from building relationships with other people, relationships which are based on something deeper than self-serving desires and goals (Kitayama et al., 2007). The focus on building social capital may lead us to contradict and abandon our deeply held beliefs through self-censorship (Argyris, 2004, 2010; Argyris & Schön, 1996). If we experience power or influence through proxy agency, we may not be willing to speak up, against the establishment, for something we strongly believe in. We may censor our own voices, for fear that we may be removed from association with people in power and, as a result, lose the power and influence that we've enjoyed through proxy agency. Illustrating this point, Palmer (2004) wrote, "When our impulse to side with the weak is thwarted by threats of lost social standing, it is because we value popularity [to the extent that we are willing to risk] being a pariah" (p. 34).

Gossip. One method for accumulating social capital (Adler & Kwon, 2002; Belliveau et al., 1996) is gossip, a common form of social communication that produces cultural learning. Gossip is characterized as second-hand anecdotes (Baumeister et al., 2004), which we interpret through the lens of our own deeply held, underlying assumptions (Argyris, 2000; Conbere & Heorhiadi, 2006; Hofstede & Hofstede, 2005). Despite being based on mere assumptions or hearsay, gossip is generally not intended to be tested for validity. Instead, we often assume that gossip represents truth (Argyris, 2000, 2004).

Through gossip, we blame people for their circumstances, and we question their character. External factors or context are often not considered by those engaging in gossip. The nature of gossip often reflects negatively on another person. We often assume that gossipers may be motivated by a malicious intent to harm the target of the gossip and damage that person's reputation, although Baumeister et al. (2004) posit that this intent may be secondary.

Gossip involves three parties: those who tell the gossip (i.e., "tellers"), those who hear the gossip (i.e., "hearers), and those targeted by the gossip (i.e., "targets"). The primary motivations for gossip tellers may be to: (a) share information—learning vicariously from the target—to avoid violating social rules or (b) develop a social bond with other individuals (i.e., "gossip hearers"). At the deepest level, the motivation for gossip may be to develop a social bond (Baumeister et al., 2004) with people in power in order to develop proxy agency (Bandura, 2002). In this way, tellers seek to benefit from the attention and social capital of people with power and influence, with whom the tellers choose to share the gossip (Adler & Kwon, 2002). Gossip tellers may also use the gossip to demonstrate their understanding of social rules or to demonstrate power by exerting social control, establishing themselves as individuals not to be crossed (Baumeister et al., 2004).

Gossip hearers may be enticed simply by a curiosity to learn social rules in order to better navigate the opportunities and constraints of the social environment. Gossip tends to stimulate curiosity because it revolves around learning from the norm violations and the negative consequences experienced by other people. People tend to be more attracted to sharing or listening to negative circumstances of others, rather than positive experiences. Gossip hearers may participate in gossip as a strategy to learn—and avoid—norm violations and their associated consequences and pain. Or, they may have more malicious motives, such as harming the target of the gossip, through defamation and other forms of indirect aggression (Baumeister et al., 2004). Gossip hearers may also be motivated by proxy agency (Bandura, 2002), through a mutual interest in developing a social bond with gossip tellers. Regardless of the motivation, both the teller and the hearer deepen their understanding of the complex system of social rules by discussing the target individual's norm violations and the consequences of such behavior, learning from the mistakes or misfortunes of another (Baumeister et al., 2004).

Gossip has also been described more broadly, as learning that derives from the second-hand experiences of other individuals. From this perspective, positive outcomes have been attributed to non-malicious gossip. In particular, vicarious learning of the culture's social rules has been cited as an important benefit of gossip (Baumeister et al., 2004). However, the nature of this learning presents some problems. First, the nature of what is learned is not necessarily validated through testing (Argyris, 2000, 2004, 2010). Gossip is second-hand—or third-hand— information (Baumeister et al., 2004). To make sense of this information, we draw conclusions using our deeply held, underlying assumptions (Conbere & Heorhiadi, 2006; Hofstede & Hofstede, 2005), leaving our assumptions unchecked (Argyris, 2000, 2004, 2010; Conbere & Heorhiadi, 2006).

A culturally learned, thinking pattern is established. Through this pattern, deeply held, underlying assumptions guide decision-making about thoughts and behaviors, yet we do not scrutinize our assumptions. Neglecting to test our own assumptions is a hallmark of the Model I socio-cognitive process. As this pattern becomes more and more established, we not only leave the assumptions unchecked but also shield those assumptions from being challenged by other people. We also use other social strategies, such as defensive reasoning, to protect our underlying assumptions at all costs (Argyris, 2000; Conbere & Heorhiadi, 2006). On a cultural level, social rules are strengthened when members of the culture follow those rules without questioning or challenging them (Argyris, 2000, 2004, 2010; Baumeister et al., 2004).

Defense of Self and Espoused Values

With the Model I socio-cognitive process (Argyris, 2000, 2004, 2006a, 2006b, 2010; Argyris & Schön, 1996), social exchanges are generally unproductive, largely due to the focus on power, control, and defensive reasoning (Argyris, 2000, 2004, 2006b, 2010; Palmer, 2004). Defensive reasoning is perhaps the Model I strategy most frequently mentioned by Argyris. Through defensive reasoning, we make statements that contain distorted information. When those statements are challenged, we become increasingly defensive in order to make some topics "undiscussable" (Argyris, 2000, 2004, 2006a, 2006b, 2010; Argyris & Schön, 1996).

Fear of threat, embarrassment, or loss of power are factors that drive the Model I socio-cognitive process (Argyris & Schön, 1996; Palmer, 2004) and, in particular, defensive behavior. Organizations' defensive routines are designed to prevent or deflect threat or embarrassment. Consequently, addressing real problems is avoided. We are so consumed with defending ourselves—as well as defending the organization's practices as "the way we've always done things here"—that we miss opportunities for productive contribution and innovation (Argyris, 2000, 2004, 2006b, 2010; Argyris & Schön, 1996).

Defensive routines are counterproductive because they inhibit learning (Edmondson, 1996). "...They also create such a degree of interpenetration between individual and organizational defensiveness that it becomes difficult to disentangle the causal roles of these two levels of phenomena. The result is for individuals to experience mistrust, distancing, and cynicism about the potentiality for productive organizational learning around issues that are embarrassing or threatening" (Argyris & Schön, 1996, p. 106).

This avoidance reduces the probability that productive inquiry and dialogue will occur. With defensive reasoning, when others call attention to disagreements or conflicts, we trivialize them and cover up our own patterns of behavior that contributed to the conflict (Conbere & Heorhiadi, 2006). When conflicts occur, the people involved tend to interpret what happened— what was said, what was *not* said, non-verbal behaviors, and even assumptions about each other's motivations—through differing, biased lenses (Trompenaars & Hampden-Turner, 1998).

As a result, people who experience conflict often have different accounts of what actually happened. Even if we do "test" our perspectives about a disagreement or conflict, we tend to talk about what happened only with people who will support—rather than challenge—our biased perspective. When we describe the situation, we describe it from a biased lens, further increasing the likelihood that others will be sympathetic. This reinforces our deeply held, underlying assumptions. Seldom do we test their perspectives of what actually happened by inviting productive dialogue with others who may have differing perspectives (Argyris & Schön, 1996).

Blame and Punishment

Defensive reasoning is often paired with blame and punishment. "At the heart of explaining human behavior are the concepts of reasoning and causality" (Argyris & Schön, 1996, p. 107). When our mistakes or blunders are called-out, we exhibit strong defensive reasoning and behaviors (Argyris, 2000, 2004, 2006b, 2010; Argyris & Schön, 1996). Embodying an external locus of control (Argyris, 1998; Csikszentmihalyi, 2003), we attribute our mistakes to other people, deflecting the blame from ourselves and projecting it onto others (Argyris, 2000, 2006b; Palmer, 2004, 2011).

This avoidance of accountability, coupled with deflecting blame, is called "fancy footwork" (Argyris, 2000; Conbere & Heorhiadi, 2006). With the Model I socio-cognitive process, one party blames another (Argyris, 2000, 2006b; Palmer, 2004, 2011), and the second party responds by jumping into defensive mode and using fancy footwork to counter-blame the first party. This contributes to "us versus them" mentality and a vicious cycle of single-loop learning (Argyris, 2000; Argyris and Schön, 1996). As the vicious cycle continues, the original problem escalates, triggering additional resentment. The problem escalates, and the parties often punish each other through aggressive or passive-aggressive behavior (Argyris, 2000, 2004, 2010; Palmer, 2004, 2011). To justify their actions, the aggressors "dismiss, marginalize, demonize, or eliminate" (Palmer, 2011, p. 13) the targeted people.

Subconscious Strategies

Hidden in our subconscious are strategies to guard against threat and embarrassment. One such strategy is "going along with the crowd," rather than boldy exercising our own voice because we fear the risk of ridicule, ostracism, or other consequences. Model I social systems, such as Model I organizations, perpetuate their social rules by instilling in us this fear of threat and embarrassment, which makes us afraid to speak up. With the Model I socio-cognitive process (Argyris, 2000, 2004, 2006b, 2010; Argyris and Schön, 1996; Edmondson, 1996), we act in ways that contradict our selfhood. Living a "divided life," we compromise what is right by silencing our own voice (Palmer, 2004), in order to avoid the risk of breaking social rules and suffering the consequences (Baumeister et al., 2004).

Dividedness begins with denial, failure to see our own thoughts and behaviors as dysfunctional (Conbere & Heorhiadi, 2006; Palmer, 2004). If we break through the denial, and the inner self experiences a gnawing dissonance for our dividedness (Palmer, 2004), self-delusion takes hold. We avoid dissonance because it calls attention to the contradiction between our words and behaviors, between our behaviors and the values we claim to have. Essentially, dissonance causes us to put our behaviors and self-serving values "on trial." Dissonance leads us to question our values and behaviors, analyzing—through deep reflection—why we are behaving in ways that contradict our espoused values.

Dissonance is powerful for igniting change, yet people go to great lengths to avoid it. Dissonance bothers us. Putting our own actions on trial through deep reflection makes us uncomfortable. Rather than make things right by committing to behave in new ways that align with our deeply held values, we rationalize our dysfunctional thoughts and behaviors to suppress the dissonance (Conbere & Heorhiadi, 2006; Palmer, 2004). When the dissonance surfaces and begins to gnaw on our conscience again, we may experience fear. That fear triggers hopelessness for reconciling our true selves (Palmer, 2004) with our place in a Model I world (Argyris, 2000, 2004, 2006b, 2010; Argyris & Schön, 1996; Palmer, 2004). We then deny the true self (Palmer, 2004) to comply with the

Model I world (Argyris, 2000, 2004, 2006b, 2010; Argyris & Schön, 1996; Palmer, 2004, 2011).

To fit into the social order of a Model I organization, we may be silent on issues for which we have strong beliefs, or we may claim beliefs that we do not hold, espousing values shared by those in power (Argyris & Schön, 1996; Palmer, 2004). We suppress negative feelings to avoid conflict. We avoid questioning. We avoid productive learning. Instead, we learn to suppress negative feelings and avoid conflict, learning which is reinforced by the Model I world (Argyris & Schön, 1996). "Undiscussability" is a mechanism (Argyris & Schön, 1996) to shield the "vulnerable selfhood from the threats of the world" (Palmer, 2004, p. 14). Compliance with the Model I socio-cognitive system is externally rewarded by the Model I world, reinforcing this thought-behavior pattern (Argyris, 2000, 2004, 2010; Argyris & Schön, 1996; Palmer, 2004, 2011).

For example, a command-and-control manager tends to reward a "yes man," an employee who consistently affirms the manager's decisions and responds, "Yes, sir!" to his commands. In contrast, the command-and-control manager tends to marginalize employees who disagree with or challenge the manager. People who exert their own voices are marginalized because they present a risk to the organization's cultural norms for command-and-control, threatening the manager's unilateral control.

When we silence our own voice to comply with cultural rules for self-censorship in Model I command-and-control organizations, we oppress the inner self. To allow ourselves to "become separated from our own souls" (Palmer, 2004, p. 4), we must convince ourselves that everything is fine. This is irrational behavior (Argyris & Schön, 1996), yet through acculturation (Hofstede & Hofstede, 2005; Kitayama et al., 2007; Oyserman & Lee, 2008), we have learned to suppress this awareness. Instead, we view ourselves as rational. We suppress negative thoughts and respond defensively to people who criticize us for self-censoring or for responding, "Yes, sir!" to those in command.

Riddled with contradictions that would not stand up to scrutiny, Model I behavior has a built-in mechanism to protect itself from examination (Argyris & Schön, 1996). Through cultural learning (Hofstede & Hofstede, 2005; Kitayama et al., 2007; Oyserman & Lee, 2008), we adhere to a social rule that makes all of this behavior undiscussable (Argyris, 2000, 2004, 2006b, 2010; Argyris & Schön, 1996). This "undiscussability" is a mechanism to shield the "vulnerable selfhood from the threats of the world" (Palmer, 2004, p. 14).

Model I: Outcomes

The Model I socio-cognitive process (Argyris, 2000, 2004, 2006b, 2010; Argyris & Schön, 1996) is damaging to individuals and to their relationships with one another (Palmer, 2004). Model I outcomes include: the escalation of unresolved problems (Argyris, 2000, 2004, 2010), pain and frustration, and mistrust among people (Conbere & Heorhiadi, 2011; Palmer, 2004).

Figure 7 shows the role of these outcomes in the Model I socio-cognitive process. Though the outcomes may contradict our own espoused values, single-loop learning guards our values—both those that are real and those that are espoused—from scrutiny.

Problem Escalation

While Model I is the most commonly used socio-cognitive process in the American culture, it is counter-productive. Model I

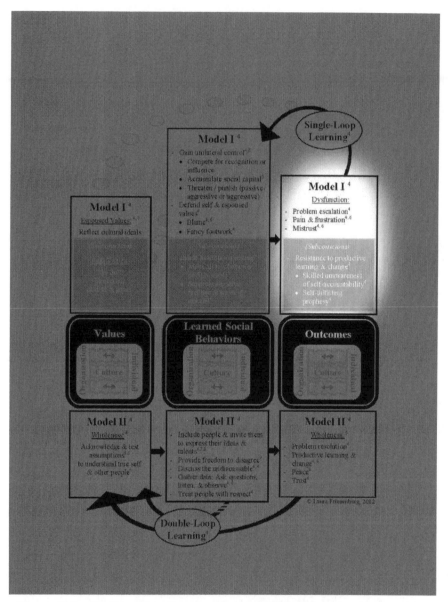

Figure 7. Socio-Cognitive Systems Learning Model:
Highlighting Model I Outcomes.

Sources: [1] Adams & Markus, 2004; [2] Kitayama et al., 2007; [3] Bandura, 2002;
[4] Argyris, 2000, 2004, 2010; Argyris & Schön, 1996; [5] Schein, 2009; [6] Mezirow,
2003; Palmer, 2004, 2011; [7] Csikszentmihalyi, 2003; [8] Walsh, 2010; [9] Brehm, 2009.

damages relationships and fails to solve problems. The outcomes are shaped by the entire Model I socio-cognitive process, beginning with culturally informed, underlying assumptions that go untested (Argyris, 2000, 2004, 2006b, 2010; Argyris & Schön, 1996; Edmondson, 1996; Palmer, 2011).

When we spar with other people, we each operate according to the same Model I socio-cognitive process, yet for each of us, the process is driven by our own primary real value: the self (Kitayama et al., 2007). Unless one party is willing to comply with the other, such as in the case of the "yes man," Model I relationships are fueled by a power struggle. As we spar with each other, we implement strategies to win power for ourselves (Argyris, 2000, 2004, 2006b; Argyris & Schön, 1996), regardless of the cost endured by the other people involved (Conbere & Heorhiadi, 2011; Csikszentmihalyi, 2003; Palmer, 2004).

Pain and Frustration

Palmer (2004) said, "All of us arrive on earth with [whole, true selves]. But from the moment of birth onward, the soul or true self is assailed by deforming forces from without and within: by racism, sexism, economic injustice, and other social cancers; by jealousy, resentment, self-doubt, fear, and other demons of the inner life" (p. 34). Rather than reject such assailing forces that prevail in a Model I culture, we succumb to dividedness (Palmer, 2004).

Palmer (2004) described dividedness as a fault line that runs within us. When you act on contradicting thoughts or behaviors driven by the culture, betraying your own deeply held beliefs and denying your true self, that fault line begins to crack. As this contradiction is repeated and develops into a pattern, the fault line fissures. Over time, this pattern is repeated. As "living a life divided" defines normalcy, your heart hardens. This pathological normalcy divorces you from your true self.

We further adapt to cultural expectations (Palmer, 2004) and fine-tune our use of the Model I socio-cognitive process. We adopt Model I learned social strategies (Argyris, 2000, 2004, 2006b, 2010; Argyris & Schön, 1996) in order to appeal to our individualistic values (Kitayama et al., 2007), while balancing the culture's espoused values (Argyris, 2010; Schein, 2009). We seek unilateral control (Argyris, 2000, 2004, 2006b, 2010; Argyris & Schön, 1996) and social capital (Adler & Kwon, 2002; Belliveau et al., 1996) and may justify deceiving or exploiting others for our own personal gain (Palmer, 2004). Characteristic of Model I, we may also blame and punish in order to defend ourselves and render the contradiction between our real and espoused values as undiscussable (Argyris, 2000, 2004, 2006b, 2010; Argyris & Schön, 1996). The true self is no longer recognizable (Palmer, 2004).

Denying yourself (Palmer, 2004) through a pattern of self-censorship (Argyris & Schön, 1996) does have personal consequences. Palmer (2004) observed, "Afraid that our inner light will be extinguished or our inner darkness exposed, we hide our true identities from each other. In the process, we become separated from our own souls. We end up living divided lives, so far removed from the truth we hold within that we cannot know the 'integrity that comes from being what you are'" (Palmer, 2004, p. 4).

Dividedness carries a cost. The fault line further ruptures when glimmers of your personal contradiction are realized. You may experience dissonance or emptiness, which may manifest into anxiety or depression. You may seek vices in an attempt to numb the empty self. These vices may take the form of harmful relationships, unhealthy consumption of food or alcohol, or other damaging thought-behavior patterns that were intended to numb the emptiness but, instead, rupture the fault line even further. "We sense that something is missing in our lives and search the world for it, not understanding that what is missing is us" (Palmer, 2004, p. 16). The dominant American culture's Model I social rules reinforce espoused values and balk at efforts to listen to the true self (Palmer, 2004).

The Model I process causes hurt and pain, resulting in expensive hidden costs borne by individuals, families, and organizations (Conbere & Heorhiadi, 2011; Palmer, 2004). Yet Model I remains the cultural default that is practiced in social relationships throughout the United States and much of the world, including in organizations (Argyris, 2000, 2004, 2006b, 2010; Argyris & Schön, 1996; Edmondson, 1996; Mezirow, 2003; Palmer, 2011).

Mistrust

We may project our pain and frustration onto others, resulting in blame or resentment (Palmer, 2004). Because the Model I socio-cognitive process mandates "undiscussability," these feelings are not shared, discussed, or challenged (Argyris, 2000, 2004, 2006b; Argyris & Schön, 1996). Instead, negative feelings are left to fester. This produces unhealthy relationships. As pent-up feelings snowball, relationships may fracture. With the Model I socio-cognitive process (Argyris, 2000, 2004, 2006b, 2010; Argyris & Schön, 1996), "social costs are immense" (Palmer, 2004, p. 7).

Operating according to Model I, we may project negative feelings onto other people because we do not take responsibility for our own behaviors and unhappiness. You may project negative feelings or blame onto your spouse or onto tangible social institutions, such as your family, church, or organization. You may also project blame onto tacit institutions, such as democracy, capitalism, marriage, or religion (Palmer, 2004).

Subconscious

Individuals who project blame onto other people or institutions do not rightly blame the Model I socio-cognitive process for the dysfunctional cycle that produces such negative feelings. Instead, we have developed a skilled unawareness to shield the Model I process from scrutiny (Argyris, 2000, 2004, 2006b, 2010). Skilled unawareness is often accompanied by other subconscious strategies, such as self-fulfilling prophesy and avoidance of productive learning and change (Argyris, 2000, 2004, 2010; Ford, 1999; Palmer, 2011).

Skilled unawareness of resistance to learning and change. Individualism serves as a major mechanism for reinforcing the Model I socio-cognitive process (Argyris, 2000, 2004, 2010; Kitayama et al., 2007; Palmer, 2011). The result is resistance to productive learning and change (Ford, 1999). Default language patterns are designed to perpetuate the status quo and to resist change (Kimball, 2011; Mezirow, 2003) "Quite simply, in the absence of people's willingness to speak and listen differently, there can be no conversational shift and no organizational change" (Ford, 1999, p. 488).

Openly admitting we are opposed to learning would violate social rules. Furthermore, such opposition is generally held in the subconscious. We tend to experience skilled unawareness that we are opposed to socio-cognitive learning. For example, while empowerment (Argyris, 1998; Ford, 1999) and employee engagement may convince the culture that these are methods for learning, they are merely masks that cover anti-learning intentions for maintaining unilateral control (Argyris, 1998, 2000). When we use the Model I socio-cognitive process, we have blind spots (Argyris & Schön, 1996; Carlson, 2013; Conbere & Heorhiadi, 2006; Waggoner, 2011). This creates skilled unawareness (Argyris, 2000, 2004,

2006b, 2010), resulting in a lack of accountability. Living according to the Model I system, we are lost and do not even realize it, as we have become so accustomed to being lost (Palmer, 2004).

Model I: Single-Loop Learning

Single-loop learning (Argyris, 2000; Argyris & Schön, 1996) is the culture's vehicle for perpetuating the Model I socio-cognitive process (Argyris, 2000, 2004, 2006b; Argyris & Schön, 1996; Hofstede & Hofstede, 2005). The protective process of single-loop learning can be compared to homeostasis, the mechanism used by the biological system as a "powerful stabilizing force" (Hofstede & Hofstede, 2005, p. 12). This process serves as the guardian of deeply held, underlying assumptions. With the vicious cycle of single-loop learning, we use a biased self-serving lens to interpret our own behaviors and the behaviors of other people, in order to make sense of those behaviors. We then channel those interpretations to guide our future Model I behavioral strategies. These strategies are designed to gain unilateral control (Argyris, 2000, 2004, 2006b; Walsh, 2010), accumulate social capital (Adler & Kwon, 2002; Belliveau et al., 1996), blame (Argyris, 2000, 2004, 2006b; Palmer, 2011), punish (Argyris, 2000, 2004; Argyris & Schön, 1996; Palmer, 2004, 2011; Senge, 2006a), and defend ourselves, as well as defend our espoused values (Argyris, 2000; Palmer, 2011). The vicious cycle thrives because it averts the testing of our deeply held, underlying assumptions. The vicious cycle of single-loop learning is like a self-fueling funnel cloud, which feeds Model I behaviors and outcomes (Argyris, 2000, 2004, 2006b, 2010; Conbere & Heorhiadi, 2006; Palmer, 2011).

The prospect of identifying and challenging our own underlying assumptions poses a threat to the status quo. Challenging our underlying assumptions threatens to expose the contradiction between our real and espoused values, whereby threatening the entire Model I socio-cognitive system (Argyris, 2000, 2004, 2006b, 2010; Conbere & Heorhiadi, 2006; Palmer, 2011).

The Choice is Yours

There is hope, though! You have a choice. Identify the areas of your life where you have Model I relationships. Are there dysfunctions in your organization? In an organization where you volunteer? Research shows that your personal identity and personal relationships also impact how you "show up" at work (Ramarajan & Reid, 2013). Maybe there are dysfunctional relationships in your personal life that you'd like to improve. Are there dysfunctions in your family? In your marriage? With your kids? With your parents, brothers, or sisters? How about in your church or place of worship? In your school? Which of these areas would you most like to change?

For the area you'd most like to change, consider how Model I is at work within the relationships of that culture. Reflect on the behaviors within those relationships, including your own behaviors. What makes those relationships dysfunctional? How do you—and others involved—seek unilateral control within those relationships? Is there blame or other defensive behaviors? How about aggressive or passive-aggressive behaviors? Are these dysfunctions "undiscussable?"

What affect do these Model I relationships have on you? How do they impact the people who care most about you? What affect do these Model I relationships have on the other people involved? What types of costs, both tangible and intangible, are incurred by the social system—such as the organization or family—as a result of the Model I relationships?

When we operate within a dysfunctional culture, we contribute to that culture, either by dishing-out dysfunctions or by being a bystander that enables others to do so. Consider your role within the Model I relationships—or cultures—that you'd like to change. Own your contribution to the problem, and make a committed choice to change.

For me, this was the most powerful learning I've ever experienced. Ultimately, this learning transformed not only my professional relationships but—more importantly—my personal ones. The process is on-going, like a lifestyle change, and sometimes you find yourself reverting to old dysfunctional behaviors. The difference now, though, is that you are no longer blind to your role in perpetuating the dysfunctions. You have antennae to identify when you are falling into old traps. Recognizing these dysfunctions and knowing you have the choice to change is tremendously freeing. Do it now! Don't wait. Let's dive into the next chapter to learn how.

5

Model II
Socio-Cognitive Process:
An Alternative to the Cultural Default

Despite the culture's intense drive for continuity and the hegemonic forces designed to perpetuate the Model I socio-cognitive system, counter-forces are battling for change. These forces for change stem from "a yearning for something better than divisiveness, toxicity, passivity, [and] powerlessness" (Palmer, 2011, p. 23). The yearning is to live an undivided life (Palmer, 2004), a life that values humanity (Conbere & Heorhiadi, 2011; Palmer, 1993, 2004, 2011).

"Only when the pain of our dividedness becomes more than we can bear do most of us embark on an inner journey toward living 'divided no more'" (Palmer, 2004, p. 39). This inner journey leads the individual toward the Model II socio-cognitive process, the life-giving, learned alternative to the destructive Model I cultural default process (Edmondson, 1996; Mezirow, 2003; Palmer, 2004).

As with Model I, each element of the Model II socio-cognitive process is shaped by the culture's flowing patterns of meaning and practice, which flow between you and other people in the social system (e.g., family, organization, society). This produces bidirectional influence between you and others in the social system. Specifically, it produces mutual influence as your underlying assumptions both influence—and are influenced by—the underlying assumptions of others within the social system (Adams & Markus, 2004; Akün et al., 2003; Argyris, 1998, 2000, 2004; 2010; Argyris & Schön, 1996; Bandura, 2002; Kitayama et al., 2007).

However, unlike Model I, the Model II process exposes your underlying assumptions to you through double-loop learning (Argyris, 1998, 2000, 2004; 2010; Argyris & Schön, 1996), providing you with the choice to change. Model II is driven by the value of wholeness (Palmer, 2004, 2011), "'bracketing' premature judgment and seeking common ground" (Mezirow, 2003, p. 60) with other people.

Model II: Values

"The divided life...is not a failure of ethics...It is a failure of human wholeness" (Palmer, 2004, p. 7). The Model I socio-cognitive process is responsible for this failure. In contrast to Model I's espoused, idealistic values that mask real values (Argyris, 2000, 2004, 2006b, 2010; Argyris & Schön, 1996) which are egocentric in nature (Kitayama et al., 2007), Model II values are fully transparent (Palmer, 2004). While Model I's real values revolve around self-centered desires and goals (Kitayama et al., 2007), Model II's real values revolve around wholeness.

By living an undivided life, there is no longer a division between your espoused values and your real values. There is no longer a division between the person you were meant to be and the person you "show up as" at home with your family, at work, and in other areas of your life. You honor the person you were meant to be. You seek to understand other people and how you can serve them by offering your gifts and talents (Palmer, 2004, 2011).

Figure 8 shows the relationship between wholeness-oriented values and the other elements of the Model II socio-cognitive process.

Wholeness is defined as "an integrity that comes from being what you are" (Wood, as cited in Palmer, 2004, p. 3). By focusing on being the person you were designed to be, rather than someone who plays the social game (Hofstede & Hofstede, 2005) and lives according to the social rules of the Model I world (Argyris, 2000, 2004, 2006b, 2010; Argyris & Schön, 1996; Kitayama et al., 2007), you can experience a sense of peace and inner wholeness. While Model I's real values focus on self-preservation (Argyris, 2000, 2004, 2006b, 2010) and self-gratification (Kitayama et al., 2007), Model II values are centered on peace. This peace comes from living a life that honors who you are and honors humanity. With Model II, you can free yourself from the Model I world, identifying how you can contribute to meeting the needs of the world and benefiting the common good (Mezirow, 2003; Palmer, 2004).

Valuing wholeness means seeking to understand your true self and the true selves of other people. "Wholeness does not mean perfection: it means embracing brokenness as an integral part of life" (Palmer, 2004, p. 5). Wholeness is accomplished by listening to your true self and finding purpose in using your talents to serve humanity, rather than living according to the world's espoused expectations (Mezirow, 2003; Palmer, 2004, 2011). "When we understand integrity for what it is, we stop obsessing

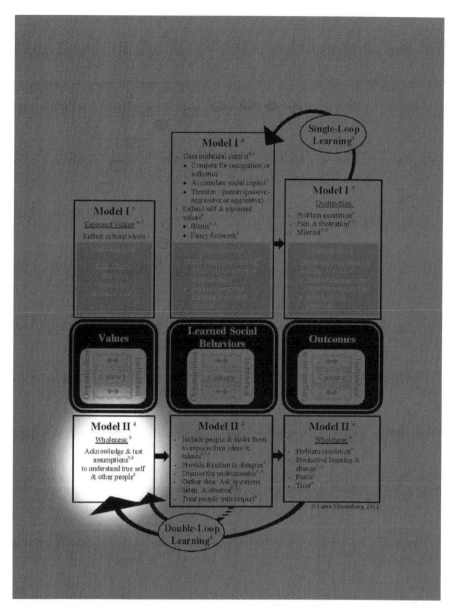

Figure 8. Socio-Cognitive Systems Learning Model:
Highlighting Model II Values.

Sources: [1] Adams & Markus, 2004; [2] Kitayama et al., 2007; [3] Bandura, 2002;
[4] Argyris, 2000, 2004, 2010; Argyris & Schön, 1996; [5] Schein, 2009; [6] Mezirow,
2003; Palmer, 2004, 2011; [7] Csikszentmihalyi, 2003; [8] Walsh, 2010; [9] Brehm, 2009.

over codes of conduct and embark on the more demanding journey toward being whole" (Palmer, 2004, p. 8).

Rejecting the Model I social game (Argyris, 2000; Hofstede & Hofstede, 2005), the individual recognizes the value of humanity (Conbere & Heorhiadi, 2011; Palmer, 1993, 2004, 2011). The vehicle for realizing wholeness—for understanding your true self and other people—is to acknowledge and test your own assumptions (Argyris, 2000, 2004, 2006a, 2006b; Argyris & Schön, 1996; Conbere & Heorhiadi, 2006).

Courage is necessary to choose wholeness because, in exposing your vulnerability, you risk cultural disapproval (Palmer, 2004) for breaking from Model I, the culture's default socio-cognitive process (Argyris, 2000; Edmondson, 1996; Garvin et al., 2008). "...We cannot embrace that challenge alone, at least, not for long: we need trustworthy relationships, tenacious communities of support, if we are to sustain the journey toward an undivided life" (Palmer, 2004, p. 10).

At the end of the last chapter, you may have identified relationships in your life that you'd like to improve. Each of these relationships operates within the culture of a social system. That social system might be your family, your place of employment, or within any group where you are a member. The Model II process is central to transforming relationships. Each element of the Model II process is important. Both your values and behaviors need to change in order to transform those relationships. For your values, conscientiously seek to better understand yourself and other people. Remain on high alert, consistently analyzing your own values and, specifically, taking notice when you revert to old Model I values. Are you rushing to snap judgments? Are you making untested assumptions about people? Are you focused on self-centered desires and goals, neglecting the needs of other people?

It is natural to occasionally veer off-course and fall into old Model I patterns, but the important thing is to recognize when this happens, so you can correct yourself immediately. As you seek to better understand yourself and other people, you will learn which areas have the tendency to lead you to revert to old Model I habits, and you will learn how to best maintain your commitment to test your assumptions. Testing your assumptions is accomplished through Model II behaviors.

Model II: Learned Social Behaviors

"Human behavior is socially situated, richly contextualized, and conditionally expressed" (Bandura, 2002, p. 276). We tend to employ all three modes of human agency: (a) individual, (b) proxy, and (c) collective agency. The agency used at a given time depends on the context, or the time, place, and people involved. For example, while you may apply individual agency in a competitive work environment, you may approach your family or close friendships with collective agency. The fact that agency is contextual suggests that agency can be changed by altering the context. One example is by changing the organization's culture from Model I to a Model II socio-cognitive process (Argyris, 2000, 2004, 2006a, 2006b; Argyris & Schön, 1996; Bandura, 2002; Csikszentmihalyi, 2003; Palmer, 2004; Walsh, 2010).

Dialogue, the hallmark of Model II behaviors (Argyris, 2000, 2004, 2006a, 2006b; Argyris & Schön, 1996), is one of the most significant methods for creating change (Marshak & Grant, 2011; Mezirow, 2003; Palmer, 2011). Figure 9 shows the role of Model II behaviors, which

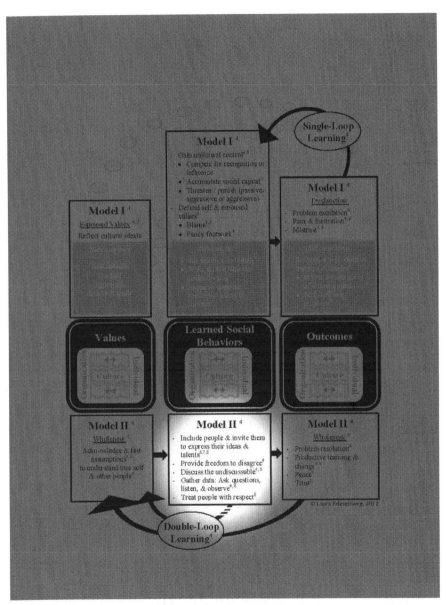

Figure 9. Socio-Cognitive Systems Learning Model:
Highlighting Model II Learned Social Behaviors.

Sources: [1] Adams & Markus, 2004; [2] Kitayama et al., 2007; [3] Bandura, 2002;
[4] Argyris, 2000, 2004, 2010; Argyris & Schön, 1996; [5] Schein, 2009; [6] Mezirow,
2003; Palmer, 2004, 2011; [7] Csikszentmihalyi, 2003; [8] Walsh, 2010; [9] Brehm, 2009.

are centered primarily on dialogue, and how those behaviors contribute to the Model II socio-cognitive process.

Dialogue is defined as "a form of consciously constructed conversation in which participants engage in a sustained and collaborative investigation into the underlying assumptions and certainties that underlie their everyday experiences and relationships with the intent of creating more effective interactions" (Ford, 1999, p. 490).

The goal of dialogue is not to debate. Think about times when you've debated with people. What were your motivations? Chances are, you were driven by a desire to prove yourself right and prove other people wrong. Maybe your goal was to change someone else's mind. Whatever your motivation, it was unlikely a genuine desire to learn.

Unlike debate, dialogue is centered on learning. The goal is for you to better understand yourself and other people by considering diverse perspectives and testing your own assumptions. Dialogue is essential to ultimately realize wholeness by living a life undivided, by freeing relationships from dysfunctional patterns. This idea is supported by Block (2008, as cited in Kimball, 2011), who wrote, "We change the culture by changing the nature of conversation. It's about choosing conversations that have the power to create the future" (p. 8).

This conversation may take place with a "circle of trust," which we'll discuss more in-depth. With a circle of trust, you do most of the speaking while a small group of trusted supporters listen and ask questions to help you through the discernment process (Palmer, 2004). Or, if the "circle of trust" approach is outside your comfort zone, you might prefer an active two-way dialogue, with you and at least one other person engaging in conversation.

In either case, Model II dialogue aims to achieve wholeness through the Model II values of understanding yourself and other people. This is accomplished by creating an environment that offers psychological safety, with open and honest sharing of thoughts, feelings, and experiences (Argyris, 2000, 2004, 2006a, 2006b; Argyris & Schön, 1996; Edmondson, 2012; Mezirow, 2000, 2003; Palmer, 2004, 2011). Openness, the precursor to the new language pattern, hinges on "*wanting* the information we need in order to come closer to the truth [which occurs only] when we stop fearing whatever might challenge our convictions and value it instead" (Palmer, 2011, p. 16, author's emphasis).

Circles of Trust

With a circle of trust, you do most of the talking, and others listen and ask questions. Circles of trust represent a rare gathering to support your individual journey toward integrity and wholeness. Such a journey cannot be made alone, or it would be compromised by your own narrow perspective and bias. "The only guidance we can get on the inner journey comes through relationships in which others help us discern our leadings" (Palmer, 2004, p. 26). Such discernment means to "distinguish between things" (p. 26) through deep reflection and self-examination, particularly as you consider your future path.

The circle of trust is based on two guiding principles: "that the soul or true self is real and powerful and that the soul can feel safe only in relationships that possess certain qualities" (Palmer, 2004, p. 29). These qualities include genuine, unconditional caring, as well as confidentiality, never to harm you or the other individuals involved. The circle of trust is a group of people selected by you, who are bound by trust, providing the degree of safety necessary for you to present your true, unguarded self.

When you identify the need for help from a circle of trust, you invite trusted individuals to gather as a group, soliciting their help (Palmer, 2004).

What makes a circle of trust unique is that its norms are countercultural (Palmer, 2004). With the Model I socio-cognitive process (Argyris, 2000, 2004, 2006a, 2006b; Argyris & Schön, 1996), people often give advice that is driven by their egocentric desires and goals (Kitayama et al., 2007). Personal agendas may be masked as well-intentioned helping (Palmer, 2004). In response to someone sharing a dilemma, people using Model I typically give advice. Such advice is driven by individualism, as it lets the advice-giver off the hook from further concern or accountability. The underlying logic behind the advice is: "If you take my advice, you will surely solve your problem. If you take my advice but fail to solve your problem, you did not try hard enough. If you fail to take my advice, I did the best I could. So I am covered. No matter how things come out, I no longer need to worry about you or your vexing problem" (Palmer, 2004, p. 117). The advice-giver simply moves on with life.

Contrary to American cultural norms, people within the circle of trust abstain from giving advice. They do not presume that they can or should discern your path for you. Such advice would only provide distraction during the personal discernment process and may lead you off-course. The goal of the people who comprise the circle of trust is to "invite [the discerner's] soul to speak and allow [the discerner] to listen, ...[distinguishing] the inner voice of truth from the inner voice of fear" (Palmer, 2004, p. 27).

The role of those who gather with you is to encourage you to discern your best way forward. They do this by asking you questions that prompt you to reflect, by supporting you as you speak openly and honestly, and ultimately, by helping you to better understand your true self. At a circle of trust gathering, you do most of the speaking, sharing what is on your mind and heart. You speak as if you were holding up a mirror. You describe the situation and explain your thoughts and feelings, particularly as they relate to the issue with which you are wrestling (Palmer, 2004).

For you, as the "discerner," the only ground rule for this process is to speak openly and honestly, being careful to avoid self-censorship. The goal is for the true self to flow freely toward discernment. Storytelling is an important element of this process, as you speak about experiences you consider relevant to the issue that is on your mind and heart (Palmer, 2004). The goal is two-fold: (a) to reject culturally driven, espoused values and Model I strategies, such as self-censorship, and (b) to discern Model II values aimed at wholeness, allowing the true self to emerge from dormancy (Argyris, 2000, 2004, 2006a, 2006b; Argyris & Schön, 1996; Palmer, 2004).

This is accomplished through active listening among the individuals comprising the circle of trust. Occasionally, the listeners will ask open, honest questions to help you identify and examine the issues with which you are wrestling. The only time that members of the circle of trust will speak is to ask these occasional questions disbursed throughout your discernment process. Ground rules of this process prevent the circle of trust from interrupting your personal discernment process by offering commentary or advice or by asking leading questions. The circle of trust simply listens and asks questions to help you lift the cloak of espoused values and to hear your true self speak (Palmer, 2004).

If needed, you may call additional, follow-up times for the circle of trust to meet. You decide when to discontinue meeting, only after discernment is reached, and you are at peace. Peace comes from allowing your true self to speak and discerning your path forward. This sense of peace is manifested by a transformation toward wholeness, by a commitment to let your true self speak (Palmer, 2004).

The circle of trust has been described as a paradox of solitary experience that occurs in community. The thoughts and discernments are purely your own (Palmer, 2004). The "community" of trusted people who gather with you help to create a space that shuts out the assailing forces of the Model I world (Argyris, 2000, 2004, 2006a, 2006b; Argyris & Schön, 1996; Palmer, 2004). In this space, the people provide unconditional support by listening and asking open questions to help you wrestle with the issue at hand and to listen to your true self. Palmer (2004) explained, "To understand true self—which knows *who* we are in our inwardness and *whose* we are in the larger world—we need both the interior intimacy that comes with solitude and the otherness that comes with community" (p. 54, author's emphasis).

A circle of trust may be the preferred approach for some people but not for everyone. For a circle of trust to meet, you— as the "discerner"—initiate the gathering, without prompting or requirement, and you hand-select the members who comprise your circle of trust (Palmer, 2004). These individuals may be family members, close friends, or even close colleagues. The people you choose may depend on which relationships or situations that you are sorting through, as part of your discernment.

Active Two-Way Dialogue

Like the circle of trust (Palmer, 2004), an active two-way dialogue is a method for you to better understand yourself and other people through the Model II socio-cognitive process (Argyris,

2000, 2004, 2006a, 2006b; Argyris & Schön, 1996; Marshak & Grant, 2011; Mezirow, 2003). While circles of trust provide a safe, controlled environment (Palmer, 2004), active two-way dialogue is somewhat riskier. Because the active two-way dialogue lacks the built-in process, ground rules, and the safety of trusted individuals that the circle of trust offers, a danger exists that the active two-way dialogue may travel off-course, regressing to familiar Model I tactics. In response to embarrassment or perceived threats, the risk is that you and the other people involved in the dialogue may resort to the cultural default strategies characteristic of Model I, such as unilateral control, blame, and punishment (Argyris, 2000, 2004, 2006a, 2006b, 2010; Argyris & Schön, 1996).

To prevent this type of derailment, the cultural norms for the ways people interact must change. Developing new cultural norms for interaction is accompanied by developing a new pattern language (Alexander, 1977, as cited by Kimball, 2011), or acceptable ways for people speak and otherwise interact with each other. To transform any relationship or culture from Model I to Model II, one focus area should be *how* people communicate. The organization should consider: "What patterns can we identify that work to support participants in productive conversations about what matters in organizations, to liberate energy, tap into collective wisdom, and unleash the power of self organization?" (Kimball, 2011, p. 9).

The Model II socio-cognitive process is one such language pattern. Organization-wide, leaders should discuss with employees the differences between the Model I and Model II patterns, acknowledging the default tendency toward Model I and the desire to shift to a culture with Model II language patterns (Argyris, 2000, 2004, 2006a, 2006b; Argyris & Schön, 1996; Edmondson, 1996; Kimball, 2011; Mezirow, 2003).

In developing the organization's new language patterns (Ford, 1999; Kimball, 2011; Marshak & Grant, 2011), the undergirding strategies are consistent with Model II behaviors (Argyris, 2000, 2004, 2006a, 2006b, 2010; Argyris & Schön, 1996): including people and inviting them to share their ideas and talents (Csikszentmihalyi, 2003; Palmer, 2004, 2011; Walsh, 2010); providing freedom to disagree (Brehm, 2009; Conbere & Heorhiadi, 2006); discussing the undiscussable; gathering data by asking questions, listening, observing (Argyris, 2000, 2004, 2006a, 2006b; Argyris & Schön, 1996; Conbere & Heorhiadi, 2006; Kimball, 2011; Mezirow, 2003; (Palmer, 2004, 2011); and treating people respectfully (Palmer, 2004, 2011).

The new language pattern (Ford, 1999; Kimball, 2011; Marshak & Grant, 2011) begins by discussing and mutually agreeing upon the process that will be used for dialogue. Through this approach, you establish norms for discussing "sticky" or controversial topics, as well as norms to guide people as they work through conflict. People are encouraged to establish ground rules for the discussion. By establishing this type of social contract—written or unwritten—beforehand, when the exchange is emotionally neutral, the individuals identify a process that is agreeable to all involved. Having made this decision in advance of the conversation will reduce anxiety about the unexpected.

In particular, the participants should agree how to proceed if they become aware that their discussion is veering into Model I confrontation or agenda-driven behaviors. They should also agree, in advance, how to bring the discussion back to constructive Model II dialogue (Block, 2000). The goal for agreeing in advance—how to redirect Model I behavior that creeps in—is that, soon, the patterns you agree upon will develop into cultural norms within the team or organization.

Transformative learning and change are accomplished through dialogue, particularly when individuals and groups of people, who ordinarily do not speak with each other, come together (Kimball, 2011; Marshak & Grant, 2011; Mezirow, 2000, 2003; Palmer, 2011). Ford (1999) described change as "an unfolding of conversations" (p. 487), which is integrated into already existing language patterns within an organization. In this way, the new conversations change the norms of the organization culture (Ford, 1999; Kimball, 2011; Marshak & Grant, 2011). Such transformative change cannot occur if silos remain intact and competing agendas prevail (Billett, 2001; Kimball, 2011). The first step is to initiate dialogue among people who do not typically interact with each other, inviting them to the conversation (Billett, 2001).

To encourage two-way interaction, Kimball (2011) recommended a generative dialogue approach. Generative dialogue provides "just enough structure to channel the energy and keeps things moving and productive. These structures are liberating rather than confining" (p. 8). Such structures may take the form of the ground rules co-created by the people who have gathered to participate in the dialogue. Liberating structures may also include organization development tools, such as large group methods like Open Space (Kimball, 2011), or the use of narratives or stories (Marshak & Grant, 2011). These liberating structures are designed to promote productive dialogue and "give everyone a voice" (Kimball, 2011, p. 10). They are designed to avoid unilateral control. Generative dialogue provides room for creativity. While the process has some structure, the process encourages freedom and co-creation among the people engaging in dialogue.

Participants have the freedom to take the dialogue in the direction of their choice. Along with the freedom, there is one caveat: Participants must follow the ground rules that they mutually agreed upon before the dialogue. In the ground rules, they should address what to do if the conversation reverts to the old Model I pattern and determine how to restore it to the Model II language pattern. As long as they mutually commit to the ground rules, participants have the freedom to dialogue about what they believe is most important. They are encouraged to mutually agree on outcomes, identifying how to proceed following the dialogue (Kimball, 2011; Marshak & Grant, 2011).

Double-Loop Learning: First loop

Through dialogue, underlying assumptions are acknowledged and tested, marking the first loop of Model II's double-loop learning. In contrast, with Model I's single-loop learning, underlying assumptions are *not* tested as people interact. With Model I, the underlying assumptions remain shrouded through defensiveness and fancy footwork (Argyris, 2000, 2004, 2010; Argyris & Schön, 1996; Conbere & Heorhiadi, 2006; Mezirow, 2003).

Underlying assumptions reflect your worldview, the framework you use to interpret experiences and understand reality. Through the first loop of Model II's double-loop learning, dialogue leads you to apply what you have learned through conversation. You begin by uncovering and acknowledging your own deeply held, underlying assumptions. You then scrutinize your underlying assumptions, comparing them to the new information you have acquired through dialogue, by asking questions, listening, and observing (Argyris, 2000, 2004, 2010; Argyris & Schön, 1996; Conbere & Heorhiadi, 2006; Mezirow, 2003; Palmer, 2004, 2011). Through this process, you may affirm your existing underlying assumptions, but often, you wrestle with those deeply held assumptions in light of new information gleaned from dialogue.

As you test your underlying assumptions through dialogue centered on resolving conflict (Mezirow, 2003; Palmer, 2004, 2011), you may realize that "the problem is me" (Palmer, 2004, p. 53). This process supports the Model II values for understanding your true self and understanding other people (Argyris, 2000, 2004, 2010; Argyris & Schön, 1996; Palmer, 2004, 2011). Through the first loop of Model II's double-loop learning process, you have the opportunity to either affirm or—as is often the case—change your underlying assumptions (Argyris, 2000, 2004, 2010; Argyris & Schön, 1996).

Model II: Outcomes

Figure 10 shows how outcomes contribute to the Model II socio-cognitive process. Through double-loop learning, you reflect on how things have played out between you and the other people involved—the outcomes of the interaction—to test your assumptions.

Problem Resolution

An organization's problems are seldom resolved in a Model I organization culture. Attempts to use instrumental learning strategies to solve communicative problems are generally futile because the default socio-cognitive process is never addressed. Simply put, organizations with Model I patterns are not learning organizations. In contrast, the Model II organization culture uses instrumental learning strategies to resolve only technical issues. For issues involving people, the Model II organization culture applies a communicative learning

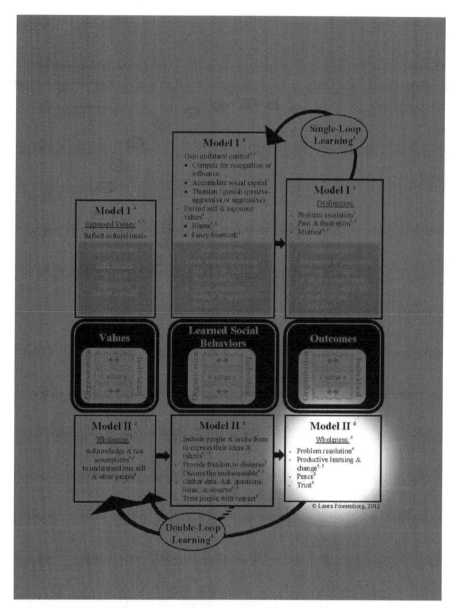

Figure 10. Socio-Cognitive Systems Learning Model:
Highlighting Model II Outcomes.

Sources: [1] Adams & Markus, 2004; [2] Kitayama et al., 2007; [3] Bandura, 2002; [4] Argyris, 2000, 2004, 2010; Argyris & Schön, 1996; [5] Schein, 2009; [6] Mezirow, 2003; Palmer, 2004, 2011; [7] Csikszentmihalyi, 2003; [8] Walsh, 2010; [9] Brehm, 2009.

approach. By "discussing the undiscussable" and testing assumptions, people using the Model II socio-cognitive process are able to pinpoint the real problems and work toward resolution (Argyris, 2000, 2004, 2010; Argyris & Schön, 1996; Csikszentmihalyi, 2003; Edmondson, 1996; Mezirow, 2003; Palmer, 2004).

Productive Learning and Change

If liberating structures are used to encourage Model II's generative dialogue and to reject the Model I cultural default strategies, you have the opportunity not only for problem resolution but also for productive learning and change (Edmondson, 1996; Kimball, 2011; Marshak & Grant, 2011; Mezirow, 2003; Palmer, 2011).

Productive learning and change occur when people or groups of people, who ordinarily do not interact, agree to dialogue (Kimball, 2011). No matter how damaged the relationships are, there is hope for healing through dialogue. Palmer (2004) wrote, "...Nature uses devastation to stimulate new growth, slowly but persistently healing her own wounds. Knowing this gives me hope that human wholeness—mine, yours, ours—need not be a utopian dream, if we can use devastation as a seedbed for new life" (p. 5).

Does the organization learn as a whole, or does learning occur only individually amongst some members of the organization? Some disagreement exists about whether learning truly can occur at the organization-level or whether learning is simply the outcome of a collection of individual learners within the organization (Akün et al., 2003). However, Hazen posited that organization change occurs simultaneously among both the organization and the individuals who comprise the organization (Hazen, 1994, as cited by Ford, 1999). Change occurs as a direct result of a conversational shift, through the development of a new language pattern (Kimball, 2011). Similarly, dialogue was identified by several authors (Ford, 1999; Marshak & Grant, 2011; Mezirow, 2003; van der Heijden, 1997, as cited by van der Merwe et al., 2007) as an essential method not only for changing business outcomes but also for changing the socio-cognitive patterns of thinking and action that are embedded in an organization's culture.

Organization change requires common ground among individuals' socio-cognitive approaches on an organization-wide basis (Ford, 1999; Marshak & Grant, 2011; Mezirow, 2003; van der Heijden, 1997, as cited by van der Merwe et al., 2007). Adopting the Model II socio-cognitive process shifts the reality of the organization and the people who comprise it. "Since conversational...reality provides the context in which people act and interact, shifting what people pay attention to shifts their reality and provides an opportunity for new actions and results to occur" (Ford, 1999, p. 488).

An organization culture that has a history of predominantly using individual and proxy agencies (Bandura, 2002) may increase collective agency by changing the context from a Model I to a Model II culture (Bandura, 2002; Block, 2000; Kimball, 2011; Marshak & Grant, 2011). This, in turn, may increase the organization's efficacy, as the organization experiences first-hand that its members did—as a community—positively influence the organization's path (Bandura, 2002; Csikszentmihalyi, 2003; Marshak & Grant, 2011; Palmer, 2004). That community experience yields trust (Palmer, 2004).

Trust

Trust stems from a new approach to leadership which focuses on building community and leading co-creation. The Model II socio-cognitive process challenges how the dominant

American culture approaches leadership. The dominant culture shapes—and is shaped by—Model I's approach to "leadership" (Adams & Markus, 2004; Akün et al., 2003; Argyris, 2000, 2004, 2006b, 2010; Argyris & Schön, 1996; Bandura, 2002; Csikszentmihalyi, 2003; Kitayama et al., 2007; Palmer, 2004). With the Model I socio-cognitive process, leadership is espoused but is contradicted by actions for gaining unilateral control. Unilateral control is embedded into the hierarchical design of traditional American organizations. In contrast, Model II does not approach leadership through hierarchy (Argyris, 2000, 2004, 2006b; Argyris & Schön, 1996; Palmer, 2004).

Instead, Model II leadership is approached through including people and inviting them to express their ideas and talents. Through this approach, the leader guides the organization culture to provide psychological safety, lifting the bondage of fear that prevents people from voicing their thoughts and feelings. Psychological safety redirects the focus from self-protection to the freedom that stimulates people to give their best to serve the organization. This freedom encourages people to speak up, offer their opinions, discuss—and even challenge—ideas, and encourage their colleagues to do the same. The Model II culture of psychological safety promotes peace and trust through community. The ultimate outcome is productive learning and change, essential ingredients for an organization to thrive (Edmondson, 2012; Garvin et al., 2008).

With an organization that has embedded the Model II socio-cognitive process into its culture, all members of the organization co-create its present and future reality (Argyris, 2000, 2004, 2006b; Argyris & Schön, 1996; Marshak & Grant, 2011). This requires a higher degree of leadership than a hierarchical structure does. While hierarchy operates according to identified goals, "a community is a chaotic, emergent, and creative force field that needs constant tending" (Palmer, 2004, p. 76).

Leadership is particularly essential in communities where deeply held, underlying assumptions, values, and learned social strategies are countercultural, as is the case with communities that use the Model II socio-cognitive process. Model II leaders are not driven by command-and-control routines. Instead, their authority is appointed to them by others. With the Model II socio-cognitive process, followers have a say in selecting the leaders they follow. The most widely followed leaders are those perceived as having integrity and wholeness, living an undivided life (Argyris, 2000, 2004, 2006b, 2010; Argyris & Schön, 1996; Conbere & Heorhiadi, 2006; Palmer, 2004).

Wholeness

With the Model I socio-cognitive process, the outcomes of people's behaviors do not align with their espoused values. This contradiction is not surprising, given that Model I strives to make thought-behavior patterns undiscussable. In contrast, Model II values *are* supported by Model II outcomes. The value of wholeness is threaded throughout Model II. In support of this value, the learned social strategies revolving around dialogue are designed to achieve wholeness. The values come full circle, and wholeness is realized as the outcome of the Model II socio-cognitive process (Argyris, 2000, 2004, 2006b, 2010; Argyris & Schön, 1996; Palmer, 2004, 2011).

Through the journey toward wholeness, with newly applied Model II thought-behavior patterns, the individual recognizes a life divided no more. The individual reclaims the integrity of her birthright (Palmer, 2004), the "integrity that comes from being what you are" (Wood, as cited in Palmer, 2004, p. 3).

Double-Loop Learning: Second Loop

Through the second loop of double-loop learning, you reflect on what you've learned from the Model II outcomes you experienced. You compare those learnings to your underlying assumptions. With reflection at the second loop, you are able to affirm or change those underlying assumptions according to what you learned from the full Model II socio-cognitive process (Argyris, 2000, 2004, 2010; Argyris & Schön, 1996; Conbere & Heorhiadi, 2006; Mezirow, 2003; Palmer, 2004).

Double-loop learning is the hallmark of the Model II socio-cognitive process because it is the vehicle for identifying and challenging underlying assumptions. Through this process, you no longer operate dual frameworks, one driven by espoused values and the other driven by contradictory "real" values. Instead, with Model II, you use only one framework. Your underlying assumptions have been named and tested which, in turn, guide your behaviors (Argyris, 2000, 2004, 2006b, 2010; Argyris & Schön, 1996; Conbere & Heorhiadi, 2006; Palmer, 2011).

6

Application
to Critical Theory

Critical theory is a field that is focused on social justice, developing awareness of oppression and igniting social change. More specifically, critical theory seeks to "explain a social order in such a way that it becomes itself the catalyst which leads to the transformation of this social order" (Fay, 1987, as cited in Brookfield, 2005, p. 7). Critical theory may be applied in organizations, developing awareness of tension and power differential, as well as serving as a catalyst for change (Brookfield, 2000, 2005; Ford, 1999).

The Socio-Cognitive Systems Learning Model may be a tool for critical theory because it explains Model I patterns, while also demonstrating the transformative nature of the Model II process. Model II's transformative process mirrors the central components of critical theory: "penetrating ideology, countering hegemony, and working democratically" (Brookfield, 2005, p. 10).

Penetrating Ideology

Ideologies are "sets of values, beliefs, myths, explanations, and justifications that appear self-evidently true and morally desirable" (Brookfield, 2005, p. 129). Espoused values can be described as ideologies. Challenging dominant ideologies, or espoused values (Argyris, 1998, 2000, 2004, 2006b, 2010; Argyris & Schön, 1996; Palmer, 2004; Schein, 2009), is foundational to critical theory. Through ideology critique, everyday assumptions of the dominant culture's reality are critically examined, exposing inequities and oppression (Brookfield, 2000).

For example, a manager may demonstrate patterned blindness with employees (Argyris & Schön, 1996; Carlson, 2013; Conbere & Heorhiadi, 2006). He may not recognize that his words relating to empowerment and employee engagement create blindness, reflecting a cloak of espoused values that disguise his real values for unilateral control (Argyris, 1998; Schein, 2009).

Countering Hegemony

Those in power use the process of hegemony to convince the oppressed that the espoused values of people in power are, in fact, true and—furthermore—that they are in the best interest of the oppressed. Hegemony is a manipulative system designed to influence those not in power to embrace dominant ideologies (Brookfield, 2005; Ford, 1999) or espoused values (Argyris, 2000; Schein, 2009).

Hegemonies are tightly ingrained into societal norms. These are behavioral patterns with rules designed for the dominant culture to ensure that they will come out on top, through manipulation of those they oppress (Brookfield, 2005). One example of a powerful hegemony (Brookfield, 2000, 2005; Ford, 1999) is the Model I socio-cognitive process. The hegemony of Model I goes unchallenged because the organization practices skilled unawareness (Argyris, 2000; Brookfield, 2005).

The Model I system is designed to be adversarial, with both opposing parties vying to win at all costs. However, this system is rigged, ensuring that people in power, the dominant culture, will always be the victors. In this way, those in power seek to convince the oppressed that it is in their best interest to abandon their own values and instead to adopt the oppressors' values (Brookfield, 2005). Or, those in power may manipulate the culture, so two oppressed groups point fingers at each other as the target of their Model I behaviors, rather than blame those in power for the oppression they're experiencing. In either case, the Model I socio-cognitive process is a powerful hegemonic system that is designed to perpetuate oppression.

For example, a manager may expect employees to own a change initiative that they were not invited to help create. He may expect employees to know how to support this change initiative and how to adjust their other work responsibilities to accommodate this new change. However, he fails to properly resource the initiative and fails to communicate the nature and the purpose of the change. He also fails to invite employees to contribute to planning the change or, at the very least, to keep them informed throughout the planning process. Instead, he springs the change on them at the time of implementation, adding to their already full workload and expecting them to know just what to do to make the ambiguous change initiative a success.

The manager's actions reflect the Model I learned social strategies for achieving unilateral control while suppressing negativity and acting rationally (Argyris, 2000, 2004, 2006b, 2010). He may espouse the value of employee engagement, as evidenced by the use of buzz words. "A central component of hegemony is the dissemination of an ideology that serves the interests of the few while purporting to represent the many" (Brookfield, 2005, p. 39). Words are powerful in perpetuating hegemony (Ford, 1999; Mezirow, 2000). Buzz words may be used as hegemonic tools in an attempt to convince employees that they are important and that they should be internally committed to the change initiative (Argyris, 1998; Brookfield, 2005).

Employee engagement is an espoused value, the purpose of which is to influence employees to align themselves with the Model I socio-cognitive process of the dominant ideology (Argyris, 1998, 2000). Using buzz words, such as "employee engagement," is one form of hegemony, designed to convince employees that it is in their best interest to align themselves with the ideals held by management (Argyris, 1998; Brookfield, 2000, 2005). However, employee engagement represents only the espoused values of management. In many organizations, managers' real values typically are hallmarks of the Model I socio-cognitive process: to control, win, suppress negative feelings, and act rationally (Argyris, 1998, 2000). These real values are simply wrapped in the guise of the espoused value of "employee engagement."

Hegemonic tools are designed to sabotage the oppressed, yet people continue to operate under the rules of the Model I socio-cognitive process. They are "blind to the fact that they (are) blind" (Argyris, 2000, p. 31). They are operating under a slew of unchallenged assumptions. Where, then, is their hope for liberation from the vicious cycle of this hegemony? A critical theorist would say that their liberation would begin by doing an ideology critique, penetrating hegemony, and seeking to work democratically.

Working Democratically

The Model II socio-cognitive process includes penetrating ideology and countering hegemony (Brookfield, 2000, 2005; Mezirow, 2003), in order to create a culture of psychological safety that removes the chains of fear (Edmondson, 2012; Garvin et al., 2008) and encourages people to work democratically (Brookfield, 2000, 2005; Mezirow, 2003). Dialogue is the primary method for the Model II process. Dialogue "is not based on winning arguments; it centrally involves finding agreement, welcoming difference, 'trying on' other points of view, identifying the common in the contradictory, tolerating the anxiety implicit in paradox, searching for synthesis, and reframing" (Mezirow, 2000, p. 13).

Using the process of double-loop learning (Argyris, 2000), you assess your own assumptions as you dialogue with other people. Each person has the opportunity to share his or her perspective. You listen to the perspective of each person, ask questions, and observe. Through this process, you consider the new perspectives that have been shared, as you seek to identify and challenge your own deeply held, underlying assumptions. Reframing, the process of considering reality from another person's lens, is essential for challenging your own underlying assumptions (Mezirow, 2000, 2003).

Managers should reframe and seek to understand employees' frames of reference. Similarly, employees should reframe and seek to understand the manager's frame of reference. Through this process, the manager and employees practice empathy and search for common understanding (Mezirow, 2000, 2003). This approach supports the Model II values for understanding one's true self and seeking to understand other people (Palmer, 2004).

7

Sustaining
the Learning Organization

"We are born with a seed of selfhood that contains the spiritual DNA of our uniqueness—an encoded birthright knowledge of who we are, why we are here, and how we are related to others" (Palmer, 2004, p. 32). A Model I culture, rife with cutthroat competition and human struggle, is bent on controlling people by clouding their birthright selfhood (Palmer, 2004; Walsh 2010). Knowingly or unknowingly, people march in-step with the culture, armed to fight each other in misguided efforts to discover who they are and the individualistic purpose of their lives (Bandura, 2002; Bellah et al., 2008; Hofstede & Hofstede, 2005; Kitayama et al., 2007; Oyserman & Lee, 2008; Trompenaars & Hampden-Turner, 1998; Waggoner, 2011). Underlying this misguided effort is a deeply held belief that in order to identify and reclaim yourself, you must achieve unilateral control and win, while others must lose (Argyris, 2000, 2004; Conbere & Heorhiadi, 2011; Palmer, 2004, 2011; Walsh, 2010).

In a Model I organization, the underlying assumption is that managers should control employees (Argyris, 1998, 2000, 2004, 2006b, 2010; Argyris & Schön, 1996; Conbere & Heorhiadi, 2006) and "motivate" them through a social game (Hofstede & Hofstede, 2005) of engagement, which is driven by elements of influence, persuasion, or espoused empowerment (Argyris, 1998; Ford, 1999). The underlying assumption implies that commitment is externally driven, and without management's Model I-driven unilateral control, employees would not be committed (Argyris, 1998, 2000, 2004, 2006b, 2010; Argyris & Schön, 1996; Conbere & Heorhiadi, 2006). This assumption is misguided, based on Model I values.

Several authors (e.g., Argyris, 1998, 2010; Billett, 2001; Csikszentmihalyi, 2003; Kimball, 2011; Palmer, 2004, 2011) have attributed real internal commitment to the tenets of the Model II socio-cognitive process, centered on co-creating organization purpose and working together to fulfill that purpose. This generative process results from each person's collaborative contribution. With the Model I process, employee commitment may be espoused, but the Model I strategy for obtaining that commitment—through unilateral control—results only in compliance, not internal commitment. Internal commitment is an outcome that is exclusive to the Model II socio-cognitive process.

Employee engagement initiatives and organization learning may espouse the same outcomes (Argyris, 1998, 2000, 2004, 2010). Yet, with typical employee engagement initiatives, the nature of the conversations and the outcomes are predetermined. Managers launch an engagement program designed to motivate people, but they often fail to ask questions and listen to the issues that are on the minds of employees. Managers' attempts to engage employees using predetermined outcomes are futile because people avoid engagement when they believe they are not heard and when they anticipate that their contributions will not be valued (Ford, 1999).

In contrast, the culture of learning organizations promotes psychological safety, freeing people from fear and allowing them to take risks to better the organization and its performance (Edmondson, 2012; Garvin et al., 2008). With this culture, employees participate in deciding the nature of the dialogue, the direction it takes, and its outcomes. The only aspects that are decided in advance are: (a) the organization development process or the liberating structure to generate dialogue, as described by Kimball (2011), and (b) the ground rules that are mutually agreed upon. No other aspect of the conversation is predetermined (Ford, 1999). Employees have an important role in making decisions based on the dialogue and in co-creating the future (Kimball, 2011). While Model I employee engagement initiatives produce only superficial learning, Model II organization learning produces an internal commitment to productive learning and change (Argyris, 1998, 2000, 2004, 2006b, 2010; Argyris & Schön, 1996; Billett, 2001; Marshak & Grant, 2011; Mezirow, 2003; Palmer, 2004, 2011).

Marshak and Grant (2011) explained, "The importance of conversations to...frame (the individual's) experience versus simply convey objective information needs to be more carefully understood and cultivated by those advancing change agendas" (p. 6). If organizations do attempt to resolve problematic interpersonal patterns, they tend to approach those problems with default, instrumental learning strategies—which are appropriate for solving only object- or task-related problems—

rather than communicative learning (Argyris, 2006b; Bullard, 2011; Gudynas, 2011; Mezirow, 2000, 2003). To change these patterns, organizations must first recognize and understand their default patterns of thinking, feeling, and acting (Edmondson, 1996; Hofstede & Hofstede, 2005; Kimball, 2011; Mezirow, 2003) before they can establish new patterns (Argyris, 2000, 2004, 2010; Argyris & Schön, 1996; Edmondson, 1996; Mezirow, 2003).

Organization learning requires a conversation shift, abandoning the default Model I patterns (Edmondson, 1996) and co-creating Model II patterns of language and dialogue (Block, 2008; Ford, 1999; Kimball, 2011; Marshak & Grant, 2011). If change efforts are only superficial (Billett, 2001), the organization will regress to its default Model I patterns (Edmondson, 1996; Kimball, 2011). True organization learning requires deep, cultural change. This change in organization culture is a result of team members co-creating new dialogue patterns that use the Model II socio-cognitive process to acknowledge and test underlying assumptions. Testing these underlying assumptions through dialogue invites a culture of organization learning (Argyris, 1998, 2000, 2004, 2006b, 2010; Argyris & Schön, 1996; Marshak & Grant, 2011; Mezirow, 2003; Palmer, 2011).

Model I Traps

So once an organization becomes a learning organization, it is "set," right? Unfortunately, no. The dominant macroculture is driven by Model I, and organizations—even Model II learning organizations—are nested within the larger Model I world. Learning organizations have made the choice to think, act, and relate to each other differently than the Model I norm. Yet, Model II organizations are comprised of individuals who have been influenced and acculturated by Model I throughout their lives as members of society (Argyris, 2010; Schein, 2009).

Model II is a lifestyle change. Though people have adopted new patterns, they are not immune to old patterns. Just like any lifestyle change, old patterns may threaten to creep-in. Compare Model II to other lifestyle changes, such as adopting a healthy lifestyle through nutrition and exercise. Even after you adopt a new healthy lifestyle, you are still exposed to old patterns of thought and behavior, and you may be tempted by unhealthy choices. Those old patterns may be especially tempting before the new norms are fully established. Old patterns—like eating junk food and failing to exercise—may also be tempting when you are surrounded by other people who indulge in these temptations. Sometimes you will give in to old patterns and will fall off the wagon (Argyris, 2010). Argyris (2010) aptly referred to these old patterns as "traps."

Sustaining a socio-cognitive change, like the Model II practices of learning organizations, is challenging. Lifestyle changes where old patterns continually confront the individual are extra challenging. Consider lifestyle changes that involve healthy eating and weight loss. This lifestyle change is difficult because the individual must continue to eat and will be confronted with the temptation to fall into old patterns potentially on a daily basis, particularly until the new pattern becomes the individual's new normal.

Similarly, people who are members of learning organizations have adopted new patterns of thinking, acting, and relating with each other, but the moment they leave work for the day, they are exposed to the Model I world. When they arrive at work the next day, there is no "Model I scrub"—to eliminate any traps that may have crept into individuals' thinking—before they enter the doors of the Model II organization. Furthermore, because people may be connected virtually to their jobs and no longer limit their work engagement to the traditional 8:00 a.m. to 5:00 p.m. business day, Model I traps have the potential to creep-in to the learning organization throughout the work day (Argyris, 2010). These traps may also be referred to as a virus (Cristallini & Savall, 2014; Heorhiadi et al., 2014) because—left unchecked— they fester and spread like a cultural contagion (Heorhiadi et al., 2014).

The contagious process is explained by the Socio-Cultural Learning Model, which demonstrates how the virus may spread as it flows between the individual and the social system (Adams & Markus, 2004). Left untreated, the virus may take hold, leaving the Model II organization—a learning organization—to revert to Model I (Cristallini & Savall, 2014; Heorhiadi et al., 2014). The good news is that, through double-loop learning, a learning organization has the potential to sustain its Model II lifestyle by identifying and eliminating traps as they creep-in.

Double-Loop Learning

The brilliance of the Model II system identified by Argyris and Schön (1996) is its double feedback loop. A feedback loop is a cyclical process, in which you reflect on a situation and evaluate what went well and what didn't go well. With that information, you can identify any behavioral changes to make on a going-forwarded basis. In this way, your evaluation of outcomes informs future behavior.

Double-loop learning has two feedback loops. The first loop serves as a mid-point check, and the second loop evaluates the outcomes. The Socio-Cognitive Systems Learning Model illustrates the role of values in shaping behavior and outcomes of social interaction. The purpose of each feedback loop is to "take the pulse" of the situation to assess whether it supports your values.

Specifically, the first feedback loop occurs during social interaction. During the interaction, you "take the pulse" of the situation, evaluating your own behaviors to identify whether they support your Model II values for understanding yourself and other people. If you determine that your behaviors contradict your values, Model I traps may have crept-in. You then have the opportunity to make adjustments to your behavior, applying Model II behaviors that align with your Model II values.

The second feedback loop occurs as the outcomes of the social interaction become evident. As with the first loop, you reflect on the situation to determine if the outcomes support your values. If Model II outcomes were evident, they likely reflect your Model II values. In contrast, the presence of Model I outcomes is a clue that Model I traps may have crept-in. In that case, you may need to make amends with other people who were involved in the social interaction if the outcomes reveal that your behaviors were hurtful or damaging to others. If it is unclear if they were hurt, you should ask them. You then have the opportunity to repair any damage within the relationship before it escalates and Model I patterns become commonplace. The second feedback loop also provides you with the opportunity to make adjustments to your behavior on a going-forward basis. In this way, you may choose Model II behaviors that support the Model II values of understanding yourself and understanding other people.

Action Research

Double-loop learning works because it is based on action research principles. Action research is a form of research that starts with the question, "How do I improve my work?" (Whitehead, 1989, as cited by McNiff & Whitehead, 2000, p. 202). More specifically, in the case of double-loop learning, the question might be: "How do I sustain the Model II socio-cognitive process?" Action research is an ongoing cycle with a feedback loop that is designed to help individuals work toward continual improvement. As a result, this type of research is practical and is often used on-the-job, with the goal to improve work-related practices and performance. Authors may describe the precise steps of action research a bit differently, but—essentially—most cyclical approaches include some variation of these steps, described by McNiff and Whitehead (2000):

"1. We review our current practice,
2. Identify an aspect we want to improve,
3. Imagine a way forward,
4. Try it out, and
5. Take stock of what happens" (p. 204).

In other words, action research is a cyclical approach that involves: identifying a need, planning a course of action to address that need, taking action, evaluating outcomes, and using that evaluation to inform future action. Action research is a tool that prompts you to reflect on what happened and take ownership of your own capacity to change. Through a feedback loop, action research uses outcomes to inform your future approach, a tenet also shared by double-loop learning.

Sustaining the Model II Lifestyle

Double-loop learning is instrumental in sustaining the Model II process. It is particularly valuable for filtering out Model I traps that creep-in. This process helps you become aware of moments when you may have reverted to Model I, and it provides you with the opportunity to restore your thinking and behavior patterns to the healthy, wholeness-oriented patterns of Model II.

You may have the opportunity to help other people who are interested in changing from dysfunctional Model I thought-behavior patterns to more productive Model II patterns. Additionally, when you observe that others who typically practice Model II have reverted to Model I, you may also help them restore Model II through dialogue, in support of double-loop learning. In this way, double-loop learning is essential for sustaining the Model II lifestyle, the culture of learning organizations.

Glossary

Culture

Culture is comprised of implicit and explicit (Kitayama et al., 2007) flowing patterns of meaning, flowing bi-directionally between the individual and the social system, such as an organization (Adams & Markus, 2004). Similarly, Schein described culture as the underlying assumptions that are generally shared amongst people in the social system (Schein, 2009).

Cultural Mode of Being

Through cultural learning, a community's flowing patterns of meaning (Adams & Markus, 2004) influence people's deeply held beliefs or underlying assumptions. The cultural mode of being represents people's culturally imprinted, underlying assumptions which guide thinking and regulate behavior (Conbere & Heorhiadi, 2006; Kitayama et al., 2007).

Defensive Reasoning

Defensive reasoning is an irrational approach that is used to protect espoused values. This irrational approach may include distorting information to protect topics considered "undiscussable" or avoiding conversations that threaten to challenge espoused values. Defensive reasoning is characteristic of Model I thinking and single-loop learning (Argyris, 2000, 2004, 2006b, 2010; Argyris & Schön, 1996).

Dividedness

Living a life divided refers to "the painful gap between who we most truly are and the role we play in the so-called real world" (Palmer, 2004, p. 15). Dividedness is culturally driven (Palmer, 2004, 2011) and is characteristic of the Model I socio-cognitive process (Argyris, 2000, 2004, 2006b, 2010).

Double-Loop Learning

Double-loop learning serves as the conduit for the Model II socio-cognitive process (Argyris, 2000). Double-loop learning is the Model II process of analyzing one's deeply held, underlying assumptions and values after social behaviors occur and after outcomes occur. Analyzing one's underlying assumptions and values is essential for productive learning and change (Conbere & Heorhiadi, 2006; Mezirow, 2003).

Espoused Values

Espoused values are values that an individual claims and often believes to be true. However, espoused values are simply ideals. While real values guide behavior, espoused values often contradict the individual's behavior (Argyris, 2000; Argyris & Schön, 1996; Conbere & Heorhiadi, 2006; Palmer, 2011; Schein, 2009).

Fancy Footwork

Fancy footwork is a defensive routine that deflects blame from oneself, often projecting it onto others. This is a characteristic of the Model I social-cognitive process (Argyris, 2000; Conbere & Heorhiadi, 2006; Palmer 2004, 2011).

Human Agency

Human agency is defined as the capacity for action in order to shape one's circumstances and achieve desired outcomes (Bandura, 2002).

Individual agency. Individual agency is an individual's personal ability to shape her own life (Bandura, 2002).

Proxy agency. Proxy agency is one's use of others' influence, expertise, or access to resources to achieve desired results (Bandura, 2002).

Collective agency. Collective agency is characterized by a group that works collaboratively to accomplish what they cannot achieve individually (Bandura, 2002).

Inner Truth

Your inner truth is the innate "core of pure being" (Palmer, 2004, p. 14). Your inner truth is also referred to your soul or true self (Palmer, 2004).

Inquiry

Inquiry is the process of questioning to uncover underlying assumptions or espoused values in order to lead to more productive action. Inquiry may occur at the individual or organization-level (Argyris & Schön, 1996). The Ladder of Inference is one tool for guiding inquiry (Argyris, 2000).

Ladder of Inference

Inferences are assumptions that are based on probabilities, and they may be seen through a lens of bias. The Ladder of Inference is a reflection tool developed by Argyris (2000) to help individuals use data to distinguish between fact and assumption.

Learning

Learning means to develop knowledge, understanding, or skill by studying, receiving instruction, observing demonstration, or through experience (Merriam-Webster, n.d., online retrieval).

Learning Models

A learning model is the cyclical process of making action-consequence predictions then acting on them. Through this cyclical process, the learning model either solidifies or challenges the learned theories of action. Argyris and Schön (1996) identified two distinct learning models: single-loop learning and double-loop learning.

Learning Organization

A learning organization is defined as an organization with the "ability to see things in new ways, gain new understandings, and produce new patterns of behavior—all on a continuing basis and in a way that engages the organization as a whole" (Argyris & Schön, 1996, p. xix).

Garvin et al. (2008) operationalized a learning organization as demonstrating: (a) "a supportive learning environment" (p. 111) that provides "psychological safety, appreciation of differences, openness to new ideas, and time for reflection" (p. 112), (b) learning opportunities built into the work process, such as "experimentation, information collection, analysis, education and training, and information transfer" (p. 113), and (c) leadership that seeks to learn by welcoming input and listening.

Learning Paradox

While the process is coined single-loop "learning," it is actually a process that inhibits learning and change. As a result, Argyris and Schön (1996) refer to this phenomenon as the learning paradox.

Mental Models

Mental models (Senge, 2006a) are defined as "patterns of thinking, feeling, and acting" (Hofstede & Hofstede, 2005, p. 3). Mental models are also referred to as mental programs (Hofstede & Hofstede, 2005), theories-in-use (Argyris, 2000; Argyris & Schön, 1996), or—by this study—as socio-cognitive processes.

Model I Socio-Cognitive Process

Socio-cognitive processes are the "patterns of thinking, feeling, and acting" (Hofstede & Hofstede, 2005, p. 3) related to human interaction. What distinguishes Model I are the "inconsistencies between ideas about action and action itself" (Argyris, 2000, p. 4).

Based on Argyris' theory (2000) and his work with Schön (1996), this research theorized that the   Model I socio-cognitive process is characterized by: (a) espoused values that contradict real values, (b) unproductive learned social behaviors, and (c) unproductive outcomes that contradict espoused values and resist learning and change.

Model II Socio-Cognitive Process

Socio-cognitive processes are the "patterns of thinking, feeling, and acting" (Hofstede & Hofstede, 2005, p. 3) related to human interaction. What distinguishes Model II is the commitment to transparency and testing of values, social behaviors, and outcomes in order to make decisions using valid information (Argyris, 2000).

Based on Palmer's (2004, 2011) theory, Argyris' (2000) theory, and Argyris' work with Schön (1996), this study theorized that the Model II socio-cognitive process is characterized by: (a) transparent values centered on wholeness, (b) productive, learned social behaviors, and (c) productive outcomes of learning and change, which are consistent with values of wholeness.

Mutual Constitution

Mutual constitution is the process by which a social system's deeply held, underlying assumptions mutually influence—and are influenced by—individuals' deeply held, underlying assumptions (Adams & Markus, 2004; Akün, Lynn, & Byrne, 2003; Bandura, 2002; Kitayama et al., 2007). This occurs as cultural patterns of meaning flow bi-directionally between the social system and the individual (Adams & Markus, 2004).

Norms

Norms are "standards for behavior that exist within a group or category of people" (Hofstede & Hofstede, 2005, p. 21). Norms are generally an implicit system of cultural rules. In contrast, laws are cultural rules made explicit by recording them in writing.

Organization

An organization is a social system comprised of people who perform tasks on behalf of a common entity.

Organization Learning

Argyris and Schön (1996) defined organization learning as an "organization's ability to see things in new ways, gain new understandings, and produce new patterns of behavior—all on a continuing basis and in a way that engages the organization as a whole" (p. xix).

Peace

Peace is defined as "harmony in personal relations" (Merriam-Webster, n.d., online retrieval).

Psychological Safety

Psychological safety is the freedom to voice one's thoughts, feelings, and ideas and the freedom to contribute one's talents without fear of retribution. This freedom is enabled by removing the chains of fear and the preoccupation with self-protection (Edmondson, 2012).

Self-Efficacy

Self-efficacy is defined as the individual's confidence in her ability to influence what happens (Bandura, 2002).

Silos

Silos are groups that divide an organization. Each silo is typically characterized by an alliance of people who have an agenda that competes with the agenda held by another silo within the organization (Billett, 2001; Kimball, 2011). Silos are perpetuated by people's failure to engage in dialogue and test assumptions.

Single-Loop Learning

Single-loop learning serves as the conduit for the Model I socio-cognitive process (Argyris, 2000). With single-loop learning, one's deeply held, underlying assumptions and values are hidden, preventing productive learning and change (Conbere & Heorhiadi, 2006). In response to the undesirable outcomes of Model I, individuals strengthen their Model I behaviors in an effort to control the situation and defend themselves. This misguided attempt to change the outcomes, instead, perpetuates the recurring Model I outcomes. In this way, single-loop learning becomes a vicious cycle.

Socio-Cognitive Process

Socio-cognitive processes are the "patterns of thinking, feeling, and acting" (Hofstede & Hofstede, 2005, p. 3) related to human interaction. Socio-cognitive processes are also called mental programs (Hofstede & Hofstede, 2005), mental models (Senge, 2006a), or theories-in-use (Argyris, 2000, 2004; Argyris & Schön, 1996).

Socio-Cognitive Systems Learning Model

The Socio-Cognitive Systems Learning Model is a theory depicting the "patterns of thinking, feeling, and acting" that are related to human interaction. Built upon the work of Argyris (2000, 2004), the theory illustrates the Model I system of values and behaviors, which leads to dysfunctional outcomes. The theory also illustrates the Model II system of values and behaviors, leading to wholeness-related outcomes. Adding to Argyris' theory, each element of the model depicts the influential role of culture in reinforcing the system (see Figures 1-3).

Soul

The soul is the innate "core of pure being" (Palmer, 2004, p. 14). The soul is also referred to as one's inner truth or true self (Palmer, 2004).

Theory-in-Use

Theories-in-use are "patterns of thinking, feeling, and acting" (Hofstede & Hofstede, 2005, p. 3). Argyris and Schön (1996) identified two distinct theories-in-use: Model I and Model II. Theories-in-use are also referred to as mental models (Senge, 2006a), mental programs (Hofstede & Hofstede, 2005), or—by this study—as socio-cognitive processes.

Traps

Traps are Model I patterns of values, behaviors, and outcomes that "make it difficult to produce the learning that is required to generate fundamental change" (Argyris, 2010, p. 83). Because Model I is prevalent in the dominant culture, even Model II organizations—learning organizations—are susceptible to Model I traps creeping in from the dominant societal culture.

Transformative Learning

"Transformative learning is learning that transforms problematic frames of reference—or sets of assumptions and expectations (habits of mind, meaning perspectives, mindsets)—to make them more inclusive, discriminating, open, reflective, and emotionally able to change" (Mezirow, 2003, p. 58). Transformative learning occurs as individuals use the Model II socio-cognitive process to test their assumptions through using double-loop (Argyris, 2000, 2004, 2010; Mezirow, 2000, 2003).

True Self

Your true self is the innate "core of pure being" (Palmer, 2004, p. 14). Your true self is also referred to as your soul or inner truth (Palmer, 2004).

Trust

Trust is defined as "assured reliance on the character, ability, strength, or truth of someone" (Merriam-Webster, n.d., online retrieval).

Wholeness

Wholeness is realized by living a life undivided (Palmer, 2004, 2011), when an individual's role in the real world honors "who [she] most truly [is]" (Palmer, 2004, p. 15).

References

Adams, G., & Markus, H. R. (2004). Toward a conception of culture suitable for a social psychology of culture. In M. Schaller & C. S. Crandall (Eds.), *The psychological foundations of culture* (pp. 335–360). Mahwah, NJ: Lawrence Erlbaum Associates.

Adler, P. S., & Kwon, S. W. (2002). Social capital: Prospects for a new concept. *The Academy of Management Review, 27*(1), 17-40.

Akün, A. E., Lynn, G. S., & Byrne, J. C. (2003). Organizational learning: A socio-cognitive framework. *Human Relations, 56*(7), 839-868.

Argyris, C. (1998). Empowerment: The emperor's new clothes. *Harvard Business Review, 76*(3), 98-105.

Argyris, C. (2000). *Flawed advice and the management trap.* New York, NY: Oxford University Press.

Argyris, C. (2004). *Reasons and rationalizations: The limits to organizational knowledge.* New York, NY: Oxford University Press.

Argyris, C. (2006a). Effective intervention activity. In J. V. Gallos (Ed.), *Organization development* (pp. 158-184). San Francisco, CA: Jossey-Bass.

Argyris, C. (2006b). Teaching smart people to learn. In J. V. Gallos (Ed.), *Organization development* (pp. 267-285). San Francisco, CA: Jossey-Bass.

Argyris, C. (2010). *Organizational traps: Leadership, culture, organizational design.* New York, NY: Oxford University Press.

Argyris, C., & Schön, D. A. (1996). *Organizational learning II: Theory, method, and practice.* Reading, MA: Addison-Wesley Publishing Company.

Aslin, R. N., & Newport, E. L. (2012). Statistical learning: Acquiring specific items to forming general rules. *Current Directions in Psychological Science, 21*(3), 170-176.

Bandura, A. (2002). Social cognitive theory in cultural context. *Applied Psychology: An International Review, 51*(2), 269-290.

Baumeister, R. F., Zhang, L., & Vohs, K. D. (2004). Gossip as cultural learning. *Review of General Psychology, 8*(2), 111-121.

Bellah, R. N., Madsen, R., Sullivan, W. M., Swidler, A., & Tipton, S. M. (2008). *Habits of the heart: Individualism and commitment in American life* (3rd ed.). Berkeley, CA: University of California Press.

Belliveau, M. A., O'Reilly, C. A., & Wade, J. B. (1996.) Social capital at the top: Effects of social similarity and status on CEO compensation. *Academy of Management Journal, 39*(6), 1568-1593.

Billett, S. (2001). Learning through work: Workplace affordances and individual engagement. *Journal of Workplace Learning, 13*(5), 209-214.

Block, P. (2000). *Flawless consulting: A guide to getting your expertise used* (2nd ed.). San Francisco, CA: Pfeiffer.

Brehm, J. W. (2009). A theory of psychological reactance. In W. W. Burke, D. G. Lake, & J. W. Paine (Eds.), *Organization change: A comprehensive reader* (pp. 377-390). San Francisco: Jossey-Bass. (Reprinted from *A theory of psychological reactance,* by J. W. Brehm, 1966, New York, NY: Academic Press)

Brookfield, S. D. (2000). Transformative learning as ideology critique. In Mezirow and Associates (Eds.), *Learning as transformation: Critical perspectives on a theory in progress* (pp. 125-150). San Francisco: Jossey-Bass.

Brookfield, S. D. (2005). *The power of critical theory.* San Francisco: Jossey-Bass.

Bryant, A. N. (2011). Evangelicals on campus: An exploration of culture, faith, and college life. In M. D. Waggoner (Ed.), *Sacred and secular tensions in higher education: Connecting parallel universities* (pp. 108-133). New York, NY: Routledge.

Bullard, N. (2011). It's too late for sustainability: What we need is system change. *Development, 54*(2), 141-142.

Carlson, E. N. (2013). Overcoming the barriers to self-knowledge: Mindfulness as a path to seeing yourself as you really are. *Perspectives on Psychological Science, 8*(2), 173-186.

Conbere, J. P., & Heorhiadi, A. (2006). Cultural influences and conflict in organizational change in new entrepreneurial organizations in Ukraine. *International Journal of Conflict Management, 17*(3), 226-241.

Conbere, J. P., & Heorhiadi, A. (2011). Socio-economic approach to management: A successful systemic approach to organizational change. *OD Practitioner, 43*(1), 6-10.

Cristallini, V., & Savall, H. (2014). The Taylorism-Fayolism-Weberism virus. In H. Savall, J. P. Conbere, A. Heorhiadi, V. Cristallini, & A. F. Buono (Eds.), *Facilitating the Socio-Economic Approach to*

Management: Results of the first SEAM conference in North America
(pp. 13-18). Charlotte, NC: IAP-Information Age Publishing.

Csikszentmihalyi, M. (2003). *Good business: Leadership, flow, and the
making of meaning.* New York, NY: Penguin Books.

Edmondson, A. C. (1996). Three faces of Eden: The persistence of
competing theories and multiple diagnoses in organizational
intervention research. *Human Relations, 49*(5), 571-595.

Edmondson, A. C. (2012). *Teaming: How organizations learn, innovate, and
compete in the knowledge economy.* San Francisco, CA: Jossey-
Bass.

Ford, J. D. (1999). Organizational change as shifting conversations. *Journal
of Organizational Change, 12*(6), 480-500.

Fromm, E. H. (1994). *Escape from freedom* (3rd ed.). New York, NY: Holt
Paperbacks.

Garvin, D. A., Edmondson, A. C., & Gino, F. (2008). Is yours a learning
organization? *Harvard Business Review, 86*(3), 109-116.

Glanzer, P. L. (2011). Taking the tournament of worldviews seriously in
education: Why teaching about religion is not enough. In M. D.
Waggoner (Ed.), *Sacred and secular tensions in higher education:
Connecting parallel universities* (pp. 18-34). New York, NY:
Routledge.

Gudynas, E. (2011). Buen Vivir: Today's tomorrow. *Development, 54*(4),
441-447.

Heorhiadi, A., Conbere, J., & Hazelbaker, C. (2014). Virtue vs. virus: Can OD
overcome the heritage of scientific management? *OD Practitioner,
46*(3), 27-31.

Hofstede, G., & Hofstede, G. J. (2005). *Cultures and organizations: Software
of the mind* (2nd ed.). New York, NY: McGraw-Hill.

Kimball, L. (2011). Liberating structures: A new pattern language for engagement. *OD Practitioner, 43*(3), 8-11.

Kitayama, S., Duffy, S., & Uchida, Y. (2007). Self as cultural mode of being. In S. Kitayama & D. Cohen (Eds.), *Handbook of cultural psychology* (pp. 136-174). New York, NY: The Guilford Press.

Kolb, A. Y., & Kolb, D. A. (2009). Experiential learning theory: A dynamic, holistic approach to management learning, education, and development. In S. J. Armstrong & C. Fukami (Eds.) *The SAGE Handbook of Management Learning, Education and Development* (pp. 42-68). London: SAGE Publications.

Learning. (n.d.). *Merriam-Webster's online dictionary.* Retrieved from www.merriam-webster.com/dictionary/learning?show=1&t=1325526270

Marshak, R. J., & Grant, D. (2011). Creating change by changing the conversation. *OD Practitioner, 43*(3), 2-7.

McNiff, J., & Whitehead, J. (2000). *Action research in organisations.* New York, NY: Routledge.

Mezirow, J. (2000). Learning to think like an adult. In Mezirow and Associates (Eds.), *Learning as transformation: A Critical perspectives on a theory in progress* (pp. 3-33). San Francisco: Jossey-Bass.

Mezirow, J. (2003). Transformative learning as discourse. *Journal of Transformative Education, 1*(1), 58-63.

Oyserman, D., & Lee, S. W. S. (2008). Does culture influence what and how we think? Effects of priming individualism and collectivism. *Psychological Bulletin, 134*(2), 311-342.

Palmer, P. J. (1993). *To know as we are known: Education as a spiritual journey* (2nd ed.). New York, NY: HarperCollins.

Palmer, P. J. (2004). *A hidden wholeness: The journey toward an undivided life.* San Francisco, CA: Jossey-Bass.

Palmer, P. J. (2011). *Healing the heart of democracy: The courage to create a politics worthy of the human spirit.* San Francisco, CA: Jossey-Bass.

Peace. (n.d.). *Merriam-Webster's online dictionary.* Retrieved from www.merriam-webster.com/dictionary/peace?show=0&t=1361656201

Quinn, N. & Holland, D. (1995). Culture and cognition. In D. Holland & N. Quinn (Eds.), *Cultural models in language and thought* (pp. 3-40). New York, NY: Press Syndicate of the University of Cambridge.

Ramarajan, L., & Reid, E. (2013). Shattering the myth of separate worlds: Negotiating nonwork identifies at work. *Academy of Management Review, 38*(4), 621-644.

Schein, E. H. (2009). *The corporate culture survival guide* (2nd ed.). San Francisco, CA: Jossey-Bass.

Schein, E. H. (2010). *Organizational culture and leadership* (4th ed.). San Francisco, CA: Jossey-Bass.

Seminal management books of the past 75 years. (1997). *Harvard Business Review,* 75th Anniversary Edition.

Senge, P. M. (2006a). *The fifth discipline: The art and practice of the learning organization* (2nd ed.). New York: Currency.

Senge, P. M. (2006b). The leader's new work: Building learning organizations. In J. V. Gallos (Ed.), *Organization development* (pp. 765-792). San Francisco, CA: Jossey-Bass.

Ten ways to maximize employee engagement. (2009). *HR Focus, 86*(8), 5.

Trompenaars, F., & Hampden-Turner, C. (1998). *Riding the waves of culture: Understanding cultural diversity in global business* (2nd ed.). New York, NY: McGraw-Hill.

Trust. (n.d.). *Merriam-Webster's online dictionary.* Retrieved from
     http://www.merriam-webster.com/dictionary/trust

van der Merwe, L., Chermack, T. J., Kulikowich, J., & Yang, B. (2007).
     Strategic conversation quality and engagement: Assessment of a
     new measure. *International Journal of Training and Development,*
     11(3), 214-221.

Waggoner, M. D. (2011). Sacred and secular tensions in contemporary
     higher education. In M. D. Waggoner (Ed.), *Sacred and secular*
     tensions in higher education: Connecting parallel universities (pp.
     1-17). New York, NY: Routledge.

Walsh, C. (2010). Development as *Buen Vivir:* Institutional arrangements
     and (de)colonial entanglements. *Development, 53*(2), 15-21.

Index

Punishment, 2, 9, 58, 64, 67, 83
Purpose, 41, 73, 97, 98, 101, 102
Questions, 3, 9, 78, 81, 82, 84, 86
Racism. See Oppression
Real values. See Values
Reality, 2, 18, 86, 90, 91, 96, 99
Reflection, 18, 27, 33, 35, 36, 39, 40, 79, 81, 86, 93, 98, 113, 114
Resentment, 58, 63, 65
Respect, 9, 84
Reward, 2, 47, 60
    Compensation, 53, 120
    Recognition, 9, 50
Rules for thought and behavior, 19-25, 35, 54-6, 59, 61, 65, 66, 73, 81, 97, 98, 115, 120
    Regulation of, 24, 111
Schein, Edgar, 9, 17, 34, 39, 44, 48, 62, 64, 74, 77, 88, 96, 111, 112, 124
Schön, Donald, 9, 17, 28, 31, 34, 43, 44, 45, 53, 56-65, 67, 72-77, 79-84, 86-89, 91-93, 96, 102-104, 112-117, 120
Scrutiny, 61, 66
Self, 2, 8, 9, 19, 24-28, 33, 35, 39, 46, 51, 53, 56, 63-65, 73, 79, 81, 82, 87, 91, 113, 116, 117, 118, 121, 123
    Inner self. See True self
    Self-censorship, 64, 81
    Self-concept, 24
    Self-efficacy, 48, 116
    Self-esteem, 2
    Self-examination, 79
    Self-fulfilling prophesy, 9, 66
    Self-gratification, 73
    Selfhood, 59-61, 101
    Self-preservation, 73
    Self-protection, 8, 9

True self, 8, 9, 63, 64, 73, 75, 79, 81, 82, 100
Senge, Peter, 1-3, 11, 67, 114, 117, 124
Sexism, 63
Silos, 85, 116
Single-loop learning, 8, 9, 43, 58, 61, 67, 86, 112, 114, 116, 117
Skilled unawareness, 9, 38, 48, 61, 66, 67, 97, See Blindness
Social capital, 9, 27, 52-54, 64, 67, 119, 120
Social class, 22, 24
Social game, 47, 48, 50, 73, 75, 102
Social media, 35
Social status, 23, 53
Social system, 4, 15, 16, 18, 19, 21, 33, 35, 45, 52, 68, 111, 115
Society, 18
    Global society, 18, 124
Socio-Cognitive Systems Learning Model, 7-9, 17, 33, 34, 44, 62, 74, 77, 88, 117
    Simplified Version, 8
Socio-Cultural Learning Model, 15
Soul, 79, 80, 113, 117, 118, See Self: True self
Stability, 46
Status quo, 66, 68
Strategic plan, 4
Subculture, 22, 23
Suffering, 33, 51, 59
Talent, 3, 8, 9
Theories-in-use, 16, 28, 114, 117
Theory, 7, 16, 38, 96, 114, 115, 117, 120, 121, 123
Thinking, 14, 16, 18, 21, 43, 55, 90, 104, 111, 112, 114, 115, 117
Threat, 9, 46, 53, 56, 58, 60, 61, 67, 68, 83
Tradition, 13, 20
Transformative learning, 85, 118, 121, 123

Traps, 2, 117, 118, 120
Trust, 9, 38, 49, 75, 79, 81, 83, 90, 91, 118, 124
    Mistrust, 9, 38, 57, 61, 65
Underlying assumptions, 8, 9, 13, 18-28, 31, 36, 39, 40, 43, 45, 46, 51, 53, 55-57, 63, 67, 68, 72, 75, 78, 86, 87, 89, 92, 93, 96, 99, 104, 111-113, 115, 116, 118
    Testing assumptions, 4, 8, 9, 36, 43, 53, 57, 75, 86, 87, 93, 104, 116, 118
    Untested, 31, 36, 45, 63
Understanding
    Other people, 9, 42, 100
    Self, 9, 82
Undiscussable, 9, 56, 60, 61, 64, 65, 84, 89, 92, 111
Unilateral control, 8, 9, 42, 43, 46, 47, 51, 64, 67, 83, 85, 91, 98, 102
United States
    Constitution, 37
Units of analysis, 43
Values, 4, 8, 9, 17, 23, 28, 31-40, 46, 47, 50-52, 56, 61, 64, 65, 67, 68, 71-73, 79, 81, 87, 92, 93, 96, 97, 98, 100, 111-117
    Espoused values, 8, 9, 22, 32, 33, 35-40, 46-48, 50, 61, 64, 65, 67, 68, 72, 73, 81, 91, 93, 96, 98, 102, 111-115
    Real values, 8, 9, 32, 33, 35-40, 46, 48, 51, 56, 61, 63, 64, 68, 72, 73, 79, 89, 93, 96, 98, 102, 112, 114, 118
Vices, 64
Vicious cycle, 43, 58, 67, 99, 117

96513319R00080

Made in the USA
Columbia, SC
29 May 2018